Change. Adapt. Rock. by WildRock Public Relations & Marketing®
2120 Milestone Drive, Unit 103, Fort Collins, CO 80525

www.wildrockpr.com

Cover Design by Teresa Muniz
Interior Design by Megan Larson, M Rock Creative

CHANGE.
ADAPT.
ROCK.

A ROCK-SOLID GUIDE SO
YOU CAN WIN AT MARKETING

WildRock Public Relations & Marketing®

TABLE OF CONTENTS

When things are moving a million miles an hour and constantly changing, taking time to pause and plan doesn't seem like an effective use of time. But strategic planning, when done right, can be a time and money saver in the long run.

Public relations is a great place to start with your marketing. Often misunderstood and underutilized, PR is all about managing the flow of information between an organization and its publics through creating and maintaining relationships.

Typically, when someone is researching a new product or service, online is the first place they go for information, companies and reviews. If you're not listed in those search results, or don't provide adequate information, customers will go elsewhere to make a purchase.

With millions of eyes online, content is key. Make sure your message stands out from the crowd. Digital communication is crucial and presents a chance to strengthen the connection with your audience and improve your brand image. Businesses need content that shines.

Social media can't be ignored when composing your strategy; it is a huge marketplace for business today. When it comes to social media, it is important to keep track of trends and changes.

Crisis management is an important subset of public relations; a process designed to lessen the damage an unplanned difficulty can inflict on a business and its stakeholders.

Wading into the waters of PR and marketing can be murky and downright difficult at times, however with this guide as your lifeboat, you can navigate the twists and turns that come with communications.

Use this section to keep track of what you've learned and your next steps.

Visit this section to expand your marketing vocabulary, understand terms throughout this book and navigate the world of PR and marketing like a pro.

FOREWORD

It's 6 a.m. on yet another Saturday following the biggest retail season of the year, the holidays. Driving into the family business' warehouse to continue helping the team pack and ship order volumes that are 10 times what we normally deal with throughout the year. Everyone is there pitching in, no matter their role. Tired, yet running on the adrenaline of knowing this is what the most successful season of selling looks like for the family-run business I grew up in.

Looking back, how did we get there? Was it luck? Right time, right place? Or years of planning, hard work, and building the demand that would ultimately lead to this success? Throughout my career of starting and rapidly growing new business ventures -- within a family business, on-my own and from within a Fortune 500 company -- nine times out of 10, it is all about the planning and work you put in to have the best shot at finding success.

One of the biggest challenges in today's environment is how fast the tactics are evolving with the rapid shift of demand creation to online channels, traditional media playing a supportive role, and every new online guru claiming to have the golden key to your success. What this leads to is it being more important than ever to ensure you have a strong strategy and plan around your own business, a broad understanding of the key channels you should represent your business in, and an approach that values speed to market with tangible results.

"Change. Adapt. Rock." is an incredible resource as both a method to understand the breadth of where you need to ensure your business is well-positioned within marketing, while also giving you the tactical tools to begin making immediate tangible progress in achieving the results you strive for. The knowledge comes from a team of passionate marketers, that give you the process and tools behind some of their leading campaign work for various trendsetting organizations.

Without further delay, it is time to rock!

Gray Rentz
Entrepreneurial leader
Co-founder & director, Polaris Adventures
www.linkedin.com/in/rentzg/

INTRODUCTION
in·tro·duc·tion | noun

The act of acquainting you with Rockstar marketing tips, which you are about to learn.

Simply put, running a business is hard. Throw in marketing, and it can be complete confusion. As public relations and marketing experts who live and breathe this stuff daily, we want to share some rock-solid advice to help you change your old ways of marketing, adapt in a challenging environment and rock your business!

All business owners want to be successful, but not every business succeeds. Why? Success does not just happen. It's not lightning in a bottle or some secret formula that works without fail. It is the summation of daily decisions that bring you closer to seeing your dreams realized.

So, if success hinges on the decisions you make right now, how will you **CHANGE, ADAPT and ROCK?**

Change
\ˈchānj | verb
To transform.

Adapt
\ ə-dapt | verb
To change often by modification.

Rock
\räk | intransitive verb
To move forward at a high speed.

The key to business growth is careful planning. The adage, "If you fail to plan, then you are planning to fail" stands true during times of pandemic, recession, hardship, crisis and other unforeseen changes. It is never the wrong time to step back, pause, plan and move forward with intention.

"Hope is not a strategy." – Vince Lombardi

Since 2012, we've been helping businesses navigate the complicated landscape of marketing and we want to help you too. Established by former OtterBox public relations manager, Kristin Golliher, WildRock Public Relations & Marketing® has worked with brands such as Polaris Adventures, Banner Health, Thule, United Way, Marriott and more.

In this guide, our team of Rockstars will take you through an innovative toolbox of solutions so that you can take your business to the next level. Here are some things you'll walk away with:

Strategy
Take your business to the next level with a stellar marketing strategy that incorporates the most impactful tools to move the needle on your business.

Public Relations
From press releases to crisis communications, we will give you a look behind the scenes of what it takes to navigate the media landscape and land prime time coverage.

Digital Marketing

The digital marketing world can be a minefield; we provide step-by-step insights so you can understand, implement and get ahead.

Content

Your brand is only as good as what you have to say about it. We'll show you how to make your content soar.

Social Media

Think social media is just memes and viral dance trends? Think again. We help you turn this tech into a powerful tool so you can shout your story from the rooftops.

Crisis Communications

We saved the tough stuff for last (we sure know how to end on a high note, huh?), but if you ever need it, you'll be glad you took the time to think through it.

As you get started, we recommend you read this entire book FIRST before beginning any work.

This book will prompt different ideas, so we recommend that you write them down as you go (contact us for templates). Once you have your thoughts down on paper, you'll be prepared to dive into creating your strategy and bring each of your tactics to life.

To receive your templates please visit www.wildrockpr.com/ready-to-rock or email us at readytorock@wildrockpr.com and we'll send you downloadable versions.

Are you ready to rock? We sure are!

- Team WildRock

MARKETING STRATEGY
strat·e·gy | noun

A blueprint to follow when everything else seems to be falling apart.

When things are moving a million miles an hour and constantly changing, taking time to pause and plan doesn't seem like an effective use of time. But strategic planning, when done right, can be a time and money saver in the long run.

We're starting with strategy because it's the foundation of all your marketing efforts and ensures you're moving in the right direction. However, you'll likely need to reread this section, and all other sections, to understand what needs to go into your strategy and find the perfect mix of PR, digital marketing, content and social media before you build out your plan.

Most companies abandon the ideology of strategic planning due to the nature of evolving economies, fluctuating social attitudes and advancements in technology. In other words, it's too hard to come up with a good plan with so much change, so they just react. However, the fact remains that strategy is still essential for businesses, especially in dynamic situations. A marketing strategy in particular can help drive toward your business goals in ways you never imagined possible.

Would you rather be proactive or reactive?

Success can be evaluated in a variety of ways, but without direction and measurable goals, how can progress be assessed? That's where strategy comes into play. Strategic planning is an important tool that guides day-to-day decisions, aids in determining growth and ensures that a company is moving forward, even in the face of uncertainty.

So, if we agree planning is the building block of success, where do you begin to formulate a new strategy?

At WildRock, we recommend starting with the ROCKS exercise. Similar to a start, stop and continue list or a strengths, weaknesses, opportunities and threats (SWOT), this exercise helps map out what is mission-critical for marketing your business by finding patterns and similarities.

To perform this exercise, we recommend you brainstorm ahead of time, pull in others from your team and even consider asking your customers for feedback. Schedule time on your calendar to work on this exercise with your team. If everyone has prepared in advance, plan for a couple of hours minimum.

During the session, evaluate *all* marketing and communication channels including public relations, digital marketing, content, social media, advertising, tradeshows, events, internal communications and more. Review the marketing approaches that are working for your company and those that need improvement. Consider channels that are not part of the current marketing mix and if they should be added. Aim to have at least five to six things listed under each category and a max of nine to 10. This will give you enough to work on without it being too overwhelming.

Rockstar Tip for the ROCKS Exercise

While you can pull in larger business issues, try to stay strictly focused on marketing opportunities.

After completing your ROCKS exercise, look across each section and pull out the similarities in the fifth column. These will be larger, high-level patterns that become your strategies or action items in your marketing plan. If need be, you can perform this as a second step at a later time, which will allow you and your team to reapproach the exercise with a fresh set of eyes.

Once you have your list of similarities, you are ready to begin building the strategy. Within the marketing strategy, make sure to include tactics and action items that address the themes you captured in this exercise as these are what's most important.

R	O	C	K	S
What 'rocks?' (Things you want to keep doing)	**What 'ought' to change?** (Things you want to change or are missing)	**What is 'confused?'** (Things that need to be clarified)	**What to 'kick out?'** (Things that need to stop)	**Similarities** (Themes across all ROCK areas)
Ex. Bi-weekly blog content	Ex. Email marketing platform	Ex. Social media contests	Ex. Print advertising	Ex. Improve social media
Ex. Consistent media coverage	Ex. Larger social media following	Ex. SEO strategy	Ex. Manual media monitoring	Ex. Media monitoring process

Change. Adapt. Rock.
WildRock Public Relations & Marketing®

Building the Strategy

Once you understand all the marketing tools in your toolbox by reading through this entire book, you'll be able to come back to this section to complete your marketing strategy. It's important to remember that during times of change, marketing strategies that have worked in the past may not continue to work, so you'll need to reevaluate your objectives and the market. A solid marketing strategy will streamline your goals, improve efficiency, provide a measurement for success and move your business forward. Success begins and ends with strategy. Follow these seven steps to rock your marketing strategy:

STEP 1:

Identify larger business goals

A good place to start is by looking at your overall business goals. These could be growing bottom-line revenue, launching a new product or hiring more qualified employees. Once you have outlined those, think through what ideas and channels related to marketing are going to help you accomplish those business goals. Three to five goals are a good place to start.

STEP 2:

Determine the target audience

Who is your ideal customer? You might have more than one. Identify and begin to understand their demographics (age, gender, household composition, where they live and income) as well as psychographics (interests, purchasing behaviors, attitudes and preferences). Note: they may not always be who you think they are, remember it's not about you, it's about them.

STEP 3:

Solidify value proposition

What makes you special? Start with your differentiators to identify what makes you truly different. What do you offer that nobody else does? Then create your value proposition. A value proposition is more of an internal tool, and, once crafted, it can help you create additional messaging points in your marketing materials.

An example of a standard value proposition is: For [target market], [brand] is the [frame of reference] that delivers [benefit/point of difference] because only [brand] is the [reason to believe].

STEP 4:

Develop key messages

You have 30 seconds to tell someone why your product matters. Go! These key messages are a foundational element to your brand and to developing a solid PR and marketing strategy. You should have three to five key messages and they should be one to two sentences each. These key messages should embody the most important information you want people to know.

STEP 5:

Conduct brief competitive analysis

It's important to know what your competition is up to. Without knowing that, you may come up with a good idea only to find out that your competition did the same thing a few months earlier. Oops! Identify your top three competitors and review and document their PR and marketing activities, including their logo, key messaging (mission, vision, about), website, social media channels, email marketing and media placements. This will help ensure your approach is original and fresh.

STEP 6:

Determine strategies and tactics

Start with what you identified in the similarities column from your ROCKS exercise. Once you have these main themes, you can take each one and create a list of tactics or action steps that need to happen to accomplish them. Make sure these themes tie into your goals.

Using our example from the ROCKS exercise above of improving social media, you and your team may determine you need to post content more regularly. To do that, you may want to identify a point person for posting content and then create an internal process for funneling information to that person weekly.

From there, you can establish a timeline for accomplishing tactics. Outlining a timeline that follows a calendar year is a good place to start.

STEP 7:

Establish a budget

After you have determined your list of tactics, go back through and identify what has additional outside costs such as printing, new signs, events or digital ads. Even estimates can be helpful for planning purposes to know what can be accomplished now and what needs to be scaled back or added to a future budget.

FEELING STUCK?

WildRock's Rockstars are here to help solve your biggest marketing challenges. Learn more at www.wildrockpr.com.

Marketing Plan Template

**COMPANY NAME
MARKETING PLAN
YEAR**

Company
Logo
Here

Executive Summary
Add here: information to summarize the plan, where you are now and where you are going.

Goals
The desired marketing results your company wants to achieve long term. Think about your overall business goals and how marketing will help you get there.

1. XXX.
   - X
   - X
   - X

2. XXX.
   - X
   - X
   - X

3. XXX.
   - X
   - X
   - X

Target Markets
Who will you be going after? The white line on top is the target audience. The bottom gray line is attributes which give key info about each target such as demographics and psychographics.

Target Audience	X	X	X	X
Attributes	X	X	X	X

Change. Adapt. Rock.
WildRock Public Relations & Marketing®

Strategies & Tactics

The strategies below will guide your approach to reach your business goals and each is supported by calculated tactics. Sections are divided into public relations, digital marketing, content and social media. You may or may not need all these sections. Note: your crisis communications strategy (mentioned at the end of this book) will be a separate document.

This is a living document and we recommend evaluating and refreshing quarterly. Keep or delete sections based on what's working best.

PUBLIC RELATIONS	
Strategy 1: XXX	
Tactics	• X • X • X
Strategy 2: XXX	
Tactics	• X • X • X
Strategy 3: XXX	
Tactics	• X • X • X

DIGITAL

Strategy 1: XXX	
Tactics	• X • X • X
Strategy 2: XXX	
Tactics	• X • X • X
Strategy 3: XXX	
Tactics	• X • X • X

CONTENT

Strategy 1: XXX	
Tactics	• X • X • X
Strategy 2: XXX	
Tactics	• X • X • X
Strategy 3: XXX	
Tactics	• X • X • X

SOCIAL MEDIA

Strategy 1: XXX

Tactics	• X • X • X

Strategy 2: XXX

Tactics	• X • X • X

Strategy 3: XXX

Tactics	• X • X • X

Budget

It's important to outline how much you will spend in all areas of marketing. Note: Unsure of where to begin with your marketing budget? Most companies spend between 10-14% of total company budgets.

Marketing Effort	Q1	Q2	Q3	Q4	Annually
Public Relations					
Digital Marketing					
Content					
Social Media					
TOTAL SPEND					

PUBLIC RELATIONS
pub·lic re·la·tions | noun

What you need when you are ready for prime time.

Public relations is a great place to start with your marketing. Often misunderstood and underutilized, PR is all about managing the flow of information between an organization and its publics through creating and maintaining relationships. Strong relationships with other organizations such as traditional media outlets, influencers, bloggers, industry thought leaders, analysts and stakeholders means you can leverage their audiences and influence to communicate key brand messages. This results in what we call earned media coverage.

There is a saying in PR: "Advertising is what you pay for and publicity is what you pray for." But PR does take more than hope and prayers and can be especially valuable when budgets are limited. Because these marketing efforts are little to no cost, the return on a solid and successful strategy can be high. PR brings brand stories to life through earned media coverage and is much more authentic and credible than traditional advertising; we call this third-party validation. However, media can be extremely powerful in helping or hurting the narrative you are trying to tell, so it's best to be involved in shaping those stories.

It is important to keep in mind, PR requires an investment of time, does not happen overnight and is not guaranteed. For example, stories are often written from the perspective of the media and in a factual way but unfortunately you can't control every detail. If you want to have more control over the message, you should consider paid ads. Paid ads allow you to put together the messaging and design and pay to have your ad placed in a magazine or newspaper, for example. You could also consider advertorials or sponsored content. These tactics look very similar to a traditional news story or article but are a paid placement (not earned) and allow you the opportunity to control the content. Advertorials and sponsored content are earned media in disguise (you often will see these with small print at the beginning or end of what looks like an article that says sponsored by XYZ company, for example).

For traditional PR, activities are essentially free minus the time you put in to get your story published. However, the benefits are endless! There can be an impressive snowball effect with ongoing PR efforts. Meaning as you get started, your brand awareness and mere media mentions will be small but as you get rolling you will pick up more and more "snow" (media coverage, awareness, interest, etc.), gain momentum and ultimately see success.

Aside from traditional public relations and media outreach, there are many other low-cost or no-cost ideas to consider when working with a limited budget or just getting started in PR.

Rockstar Tips for Low-Cost/No-Cost PR Ideas

Draft a press release and distribute news to media.

Many newsrooms have editor contact information on their website and/or a submission form for news tips and press releases. We've included an easy press release template and example later in this section so you know what to include and can format it to journalist expectations with AP Style.

Create an engaging social media post to tell your story (see social media section for a ton of tips to get you started).

With the continued merging of PR and social media, online channels have become another great platform for brand publishing and storytelling.

Distribute an email newsletter (more to come in the email marketing section).

Is your email list under 2,000? MailChimp offers free resources and even basic email marketing templates so you can send out a polished campaign.

Host a contest or giveaway.

These can help you collect email addresses for future email campaigns, engage with your customers in new ways and get people interested in new products or services. (Once again, see the social media section for a ton of tips to get you started).

Rockstar Tips for Low-Cost/No-Cost PR Ideas

Share content on your blog.

Use a blog to promote what makes your brand special and broadcast your news. Blogs also help build your search engine optimization (SEO) credibility when you use relevant keywords (more to come on this topic in the content section).

Partner with bloggers or influencers to share your story.

Reach out to find out what they are working on and talk about what story ideas you offer that speak to their audience. Can you offer them a product/service to share with their fans?

Seek out co-marketing opportunities for cross-promotion.

Think about asking like-minded brands to share content on your business, maybe through their email marketing or social media channels. In turn, you promote their business through your channels.

Comment and share industry articles on social media to establish a presence and credibility.

Tap into what's happening in your market by keeping a pulse on your industry's trade publications, professional organizations, events, etc. You can do this from your business channels, but also your personal channels too.

Attend networking events for word-of-mouth marketing.

Tap into your local chamber of commerce or industry groups to get your name out there. Collect business cards and follow up with everyone personally via email and connect on LinkedIn.

Leverage your network (friends, family, previous co-workers, neighbors, etc.) and ask for help to share your news on their channels.

As you grow your LinkedIn connections (or other platforms), there are great opportunities to reach out to people personally to ask for their support.

See the "who you know" exercise later in this section for some great starting points to get you heading in the right direction to build a list of a least 100 people.

Create internal messaging points for employees.

Ensure you are all on the same page for clear and consistent brand messaging, plus having your employees share with their networks is free advertising.

PR Tools

Every profession has its tools of the trade and PR is no different. Just like a carpenter has a toolbox for construction, a PR pro has a lot of different tools in their toolbox to help distribute, track, evaluate and manage public relations efforts. When establishing a foundation, you should consider investing in these key basics:

 ## Media database

If PR is who you know, think of your media database as your little black book. A media database, often subscription or fee-based, is a PR super-tool. It is a resource that manages thousands of contacts in the news media industry such as journalists, reporters, editors, producers and more. Some even include influencer contacts. You have important news to tell but who do you send it to? A media database is where you go to answer that question. You can certainly do it the old-fashioned way, with online research and calls to newsrooms, but that takes time – especially if you have news to distribute on a national or global scale. Not to mention, media contacts move around a lot or freelance for multiple outlets and contact information changes which makes it hard to keep track. A media database streamlines and simplifies contact research. Some of the major players are Cision (cison.com) and Muck Rack (muckrack.com) but there are others to consider based on your needs and budget.

 ## CRM/PRM

Keep your ducks in a row with a customer relationship management (CRM) tool or, for PR, a public relations management (PRM) tool. This will help organize your media contacts and track outreach efforts in one place. This is especially helpful when multiple people are working in media relations so each person can easily reference what news has been sent to what contacts to avoid overlap and inundating. Some paid PRM tools even track success rate with contacts so you can focus on those that are most interested in your brand. You can create your own system with Excel spreadsheets or GoogleDocs (google.com/docs/about) or invest in something more sophisticated such as Propel (propelmypr.com).

Distribution via wire

To take your news distribution to the next level, consider a wire distribution through a service such as PR Newswire (prnewswire.com) or Business Wire (businesswire.com). For a fee (generally based on word count of your press release plus added media assets, such as photos and videos), these platforms deliver your press release directly into newsrooms using a multi-channel network that includes access to organizations like the Associated Press, Dow Jones, Thomson Reuters, Bloomberg and more. They can be costly but also can help you target key outlets and get some instant visibility with less work than sending press releases to individual media contacts. They are especially beneficial when you need to get news out quickly, accurately and to a large audience (think executive changes, mergers, acquisitions, meeting SEC requirements with public announcements, etc.). Newswires also create referral traffic to your website as you will instantaneously have backlinks the moment the release crosses the wire. Newswires, however, are not intended to replace good old-fashioned media relationship building, as they typically take your press release verbatim and post online. While it may happen, it's unlikely you'll get a call directly from the media. It's more of a quick hit, then it's done. Building media relationships is the most impactful PR effort so far.

Distribution via pitching

As mentioned, the most beneficial way to get your news out there is to establish personal relationships with the media. This allows you to get inside their head and seek out what's important to them, understand their readers/audience, know what's coming up on their editorial calendar and find out how you can help them. LinkedIn (linkedin.com) is a great way to connect with media, read their articles and get in front of trends to help you establish a thought leadership reputation and credibility to be quoted. Ask good questions before coming right out with what you need, see what they are interested in and craft your story angle from there. Twitter (twitter.com) is another way to monitor what media is working on and engage with them. When you are ready to pitch, continue to ask yourself, "What's in it for them?" Remember they are people too, so respect is key and creating long-term relationships will help you both!

Monitoring

This tool is your eyes and ears. In PR, what you don't know can hurt you. The activity of monitoring what is said about your brand in the media is a must. In addition to the earned media that results from your proactive outreach, there may also be coverage happening organically. You should be aware of the public's perception of your brand – positive and negative. Either way, it is best to have your voice be part of the narrative. If you are monitoring what is published, you have a better chance of speaking up quickly and getting involved, particularly in a crisis. Monitoring positive coverage that you were not expecting is a good opportunity to reach out, thank the writer and start to establish a relationship for future stories. Another important advantage of monitoring news is to keep tabs on what your competitors are doing. You can track share of voice to better understand how your news coverage compares to your competitors and gauge your brand visibility in the industry. There are free tools to use for monitoring such as Google Alerts (google.com/alerts) and Talkwalker Alerts (talkwalker.com/alerts) or you can search manually using a search engine or go directly to an outlet's website. For more robust monitoring (with a cost), consider services such as Critical Mention (criticalmention.com) or Meltwater (meltwater.com).

Reporting

Reporting helps prove that all your hard work in PR is worth it, or possibly that your tactics need adjustment and improvement. Before any PR campaign, you should establish reporting metrics (and include those in your overall marketing strategy). Typically, these will include circulation/online readership; number of placements; coverage type (feature, mention, press release, etc.); sentiment (positive, neutral, negative); share of voice among competitors; key message inclusion; wish list outlet placement; call to action (visit website, call, book, etc.) and brand asset feature (logo, image, video, spokesperson quotes, etc.). These can be used as key performance indicators to gauge success. Most monitoring services will include reporting but there are separate tools available that are more cost-effective if you are doing monitoring on your own and just need a way to compile reporting information into a nicely branded showpiece. Tools such as CoverageBook (coveragebook.com) allow you to create a report in a matter of minutes and automatically include metrics such as unique monthly views, coverage views, social shares and domain authority (which can save hours of manual reporting). See Tracking Value in the social media section for more information on how you can report out on PR and other marketing efforts.

The Press Release

One of the most fundamental "tools" in PR is the press release. This is used to communicate important news from your company to the media. Not everything is newsworthy though, so you need to use this tool for the right announcements. Journalists are taught that, "When a dog bites a man, that is not news because it happens so often. But if a man bites a dog, that is news." This is the kind of angle they will be looking for, so you need to identify what is new, unique, different or compelling about what you have to share.

Before drafting a press release, ask yourself, "Is my story newsworthy?" Here are some tips to evaluate newsworthiness:

- **Impact:** How will the news affect the audience? Is this something the public needs to know for a significant reason? How will their lives be improved or changed?

- **Timeliness:** How recent is the information? Why do you need to share now? Media is hungry for content but it can't be old news. In today's instant and internet-enabled world, "old" is an extremely relative term and will vary by the news outlet.

- **Proximity:** Why should media care? Depending on where the outlet is based, and whether they cover local or national news, this may change their geographic focus.

- **Novelty:** Anything unusual about this announcement? Nothing turns heads like the extraordinary or unusual.

- **Conflict:** Are there different sides to this news? Controversy does sell but approach this with caution.

- **Human Interest:** Does this have a good story people will want to hear about? People like to hear about people, especially good people doing good things.

- **Celebrity:** Does this involve anyone notable? Society has a never-ending obsession with the famous, or infamous.

Once you're ready with your news and you have a strong angle in mind, use an inverted pyramid approach to structure your press release. An inverted pyramid illustrates how to organize your information so that the most important messages are at the beginning followed by supporting details. This structure allows the media to quickly assess your news and get the main points of the press release.

Inverted Pyramid Writing Structure

Most important info - Why should I care? (headline and first paragraph should have everything a reader needs to understand the story).

Somewhat important info - Hmm, that's interesting I'll read on (isn't essential for understanding of the story).

Nice to have - I have the attention span of a puppy. If I make it here it's a miracle (this is boilerplate info, and rounds out a conclusion to your story).

To make things easy, you can use the template on the next page to fill in your press release details.

FOR IMMEDIATE RELEASE

Media Contact:
Your name
YourEmail@email.com
Phone number

Catchy headline goes here

Brief sentence to further explain and support announcement

CITY, St. (Month Day, Year) – Intro: Important information about who, what, when, why, how. Remember, the most critical info goes here. Readers typically only make it to the headline, subhead and the first paragraph then stop.

P1: Background information on the organization, what you do and more details on the announcement.

P2: Explain why this is important, what is newsworthy, what problem does this solve, etc.?

P3: Insert a quote.

P4: Provide a call to action (for more information visit, to schedule an appointment call, etc.)

About: Include boilerplate information (company about us).

###

If you're unsure of what this might look like, here's a high-level example based on a fictional company.

Best Boutique expands with personal shopping services
Personal shoppers select styles and revamp look

FORT COLLINS, Colo. (May 25, 2020) – Best Boutique, known throughout Colorado for the leading contemporary women's fashion designs, is expanding later this month with the addition of personal shopping services. By appointment only, the personal shopping services will complement Best Boutique's new collection of hippie-chic clothes with the ability for customers to have assistance to discover fresh, new custom looks.

Based in Fort Collins, Best Boutique has locations in Denver, Aurora and Broomfield and will offer personal shopping services via online signup for all four locations. The online signup includes a quick style and size assessment that allows the personal shopper to begin research in advance of the appointment.

Once the appointment is scheduled, the personal shopper will meet the customer at one of the Best Boutique locations with pre-selected outfits for the customer to choose from. The session then includes advice and additional style selections until the ideal look is achieved.

The idea for a personal shopper came directly from customer feedback. Best Boutique surveyed customers last year between May and June and found that over 70 percent of customers said if offered the option for a personal shopper that would jump on the opportunity.

"The request for personal shoppers from our customers was overwhelming," Violet Robinson said, president of Best Boutique. "This is just another great example of how we continue to create a unique experience at our boutiques by offering customers new styles tailored just for them."

Personal shopper appointments depend on the length of time and are priced starting at $75 for one-half hour. To learn more or to sign up, visit www.bestboutique.com/personalshopper.

About: Best Boutique prides itself on offering women of all shapes and sizes the latest in casual clothing with flair. Established in 2015, Best Boutique started with its flagship store in Fort Collins and has now grown to four retail locations. With a mission to make fashion fun and easy, Best Boutique has continued to add new services such as its signature Ladies Night every Thursday.

###

Rockstar Tips for Grammar and Style

Follow The Associated Press Stylebook guidelines for grammar and style usage. More information can be found at APStylebook.com.

Press Release Checklist

When writing a press release, here are the best practices to follow:

☐ Include "For Immediate Release" or an embargo date if the news needs to be held before publishing.

- An embargo date gives media advance notice on the announcement and allows them to work ahead on stories, under the agreement they will not publish until that specified date/time.

☐ Contact information either at the top or bottom (include name, title, email, phone and cell).

☐ Eye-catching headline.

☐ Dateline for where the news is coming from (typically the location of the company's headquarters).

☐ Inverted pyramid writing structure (see diagram on page 31).

- Most important information in the first paragraph.
- Supporting details to follow.
- The body should be short and sweet. One idea per paragraph.
- Quotes should be relevant and to the point.

☐ Use "- more -" when continuing to another page.

☐ Use "###" to signify the end of the press release.

☐ Include company boilerplate/about us.

☐ Do I have a solid news hook?

☐ Did I follow AP Style?

☐ Do I have all appropriate parties approved the press release?

☐ What is the timeline?
- When does the press release need to go out?
- Do I have enough lead time?
- After I send my press release, when will I follow up?

☐ What is the overall goal?
- What should the PR campaign accomplish?
- How will I evaluate success?

☐ Who is the audience?
- Do I have my media list built and do I know what the media members write about?

☐ Do I have custom pitches drafted to send with my press release?

☐ Am I attaching a photo or video?
- Is the photo or video high resolution but not too big that it won't send?

Visit www.wildrockpr.com/ready-to-rock or contact us at readytorock@wildrockpr.com for your FREE printable templates, checklists and forms to take notes as you read.

Change. Adapt. Rock.
WildRock Public Relations & Marketing®

Press Release Follow Up

After your press release goes out to the world, the work does not stop. In fact, in many ways, it is just beginning. You have cast the line and now you are ready for something to bite. Here is what you need to do to follow up and reel in those media placements:

- Depending on your news, you will want to follow up anywhere between 24 to 72 hours after sending the press release.
  - For more time-sensitive announcements, it's appropriate to follow up quickly.
- First, follow up with an email that is short and sweet.
  - Our recommendation is to forward the original pitch and include the message "Any interest in the news below?"
  - If you reply to the original email, it will look as if you and this contact have already been in communication and that can be deceiving, which is a turn off for media.
- If you don't hear back after the first follow up, you can email again but after that be very cautious of how often you are reaching out.
  - You do not want to annoy or pester the media; keep in mind they get hundreds of pitches and press releases every day. If they are interested, you will typically get a response from the first one or two emails.
  - Preferences vary on phone calls – some media contacts don't mind them while others would prefer not to be contacted that way. If you are using a database like Cision, you can research their communication preferences to know if that is appropriate.
  - With additional follow ups, it can be useful to include a timely update such as, "We have a new development in this news that I thought might interest you..." Or, "I noticed your recent story on this topic that would relate to what we are doing..."

- If you do not receive any response or interest was lower than you hoped, you may need to move to an alternative plan which might include:
  - Expanding your media list. Perhaps you started with a smaller pool that was very niche. You will now need to consider broader outlets or contacts, and even non-traditional mediums such as podcasts or blogs.
  - Revisiting your news angle. Go back and evaluate the newsworthiness of your announcement. Is there another approach you can take? Can you apply your news to what's already trending in the media? This concept is called "newsjacking" and can be very successful if done appropriately.
- One of the most important things to keep in mind when working with media is timely response. When you do hear from someone after your announcement, make sure you get back to them as quickly as possible.
  - If you need to seek information to answer a question or check on schedules to coordinate an interview, let them know you are working on it and you will get back to them.
  - Also, it's very important to ask if they have a deadline so you can respect that.
  - You should also ask them when the story is expected to publish so you don't miss it.
- After a press release goes out, you should increase your monitoring to make sure you don't miss any placements.
  - There may be media who take your release and run with it, without letting you know. This is great, but it's always good to track those and send a thank you to the writer.

Change. Adapt. Rock.
WildRock Public Relations & Marketing®

- If through your monitoring you come across any negative articles or inaccuracies, you should address them right away with the media contact. The best-case scenario would be that they revise the article to be more favorable, but that is typically only the case if the information truly is not accurate. Keep in mind, they have editorial freedom to present information as they see it.

- Finally, keep track of all placements and save for your reporting. You may be using an automatic tool like Meltwater or Critical Mention referenced previously, but if not, this is extremely important so you can evaluate and showcase results.

PR is typically more of a marathon than a sprint, especially when working with long-lead publications that work on content three to six months in advance. Some stories will take longer than others but have patience, keep engaged with the media you are working with and don't forget to follow up. Most earned media coverage is a result of persistent follow up!

DID WE LOSE YOU BETWEEN THE "P" OR THE "R?"

WildRock's Rockstars are here to help solve your biggest PR challenges. Learn more at www.wildrockpr.com.

Community Sponsorships & Events

While community sponsorships often fall under the event category, they are also a public relations tactic that allows you to get in front of target audiences for a fee without the full cost and effort of exhibiting at a tradeshow or running an event yourself.

Getting your name out there and building your brand can be as simple as a banner or booth at an event. Events such as fun runs and festivals come with a built-in audience ready to help you create brand recognition with customers. If you haven't tried your hand at events, they can be well worth it, but they are time-consuming and require dedication from a detail-oriented person to make them a success (see our helpful checklist if you are going down the event road, there is a lot to consider).

For purposes of this context, we are focusing on community sponsorships to garner brand exposure. If you can sponsor an event with a fee or in-kind donation, the first step is to identify what events your target audience will attend. Look at local community calendars to discover when these events are held and what organizations are planning them. Many companies sponsor events and wonder why they aren't successful in reaching potential customers, so ensuring your target audience will be there is critical. Don't waste time, money or energy sponsoring something that doesn't reach them.

Depending on your sponsorship level, you may receive:

- Company name and logo on event marketing materials.
- Company name, logo and website link on the event website.
- Logo on event T-shirts.
- Mentions and shoutouts on social media.
- Inclusion in email marketing.
- Presence on event banners, whether hung at an actual event or a graphic on a website.
- Speaking opportunities at the event.
- Ability to provide branded swag.

- Free passes to the event, typically reserved for a higher level of sponsorship.
- VIP access, typically reserved for a higher level of sponsorship.
- Naming rights, typically reserved for a higher level of sponsorship.
- Access to participant contact information.
  - Note: This may not be applicable at non-profit events but could be at larger tradeshows or conferences.

When you've settled on your sponsorship level, we recommend signing a contract so that all parties understand how the partnership will work. To capitalize on the sponsorship, provide the event organizers a hi-resolution version of your logo along with a public-facing description of your business that can be used in marketing materials. You should also receive the event logo and description to cross-promote on your channels as well.

It's a good practice to continually follow up with event organizers to ensure they are following through with sponsorship benefits and you're able to take advantage of any opportunities that may arise. If you can speak or present during the event, prepare talking points in advance. Remember to keep it high level, thanking the attendees for their participation and reiterating your value proposition.

Leverage the event itself by participating as much as possible. Ideas include live social media posts throughout the day, including use of the event hashtags (see the social media section for more information), or an email follow-up to the leads you collect at the event. Attendance on the day of the event can also be a great place to make new business connections and meet customers face-to-face. Remember, this is an opportunity to strengthen your brand by showing your goodwill and community support while also being in front of a captive audience.

Some sponsorships of non-profit organizations and events may be tax-deductible. Be sure to check with your tax advisor when filing taxes to further leverage your marketing spend and ask for a tax receipt following payment to keep for your records.

Event Planning Template and Checklist

If you decide you want to plan your own event, there are a ton of details to keep track of. To help organize all activities, use this planning template and checklist so nothing is overlooked.

Event Date: _____

Event Time: _____

Location: _____

Lead Contact: _____

3-6 Months Before the Event

- [ ] Event goals & outline
    - [ ] Determine what you want to accomplish
    - [ ] Establish a budget
    - [ ] Designate fixed costs and variable costs
    - [ ] Identify the target audience(s)
    - [ ] Develop a theme and name of the event to carry through all promotions
    - [ ] Brainstorm unique appeal
        - [ ] What will grab interest and attention?
        - [ ] Any special offers and/or gifts to give out?
    - [ ] Set the date and time of the event
    - [ ] Double-check local event calendars to avoid conflicting dates
    - [ ] Draft messaging and description of the event
    - [ ] Confirm if and what the registration fee will be and how attendees will register
- [ ] Venue
    - [ ] Select venue

- ☐ Review, sign and return contract
- ☐ Estimated attendance: _____
- ☐ Date to cancel event without penalty: _____
- ☐ Deposit amount and date due (if required): _____
- ☐ Date to provide final attendance numbers: _____
- ☐ Arrange set up and space needs
- ☐ Map out seating, stations, registration area, etc.
- ☐ Arrange for equipment and AV
  - Obtain list of options and pricing (microphones, podium, screen, etc.)
  - Confirm needs and place order
- ☐ Arrange photography (if applicable: professional or volunteer)
- ☐ Research catering options
  - Review menu selections
  - Consider special dietary needs
  - Bar/beverages (determine complimentary or cash)
- ☐ Coordinate rentals (if applicable)
- ☐ Select entertainment/activities
  - Musicians or other
- ☐ Consider decoration needs
  - Floral arrangements, balloons, etc.
  - Signage
- ☐ Develop a draft of event agenda
  - ☐ Timing
  - ☐ Room locations
  - ☐ Speakers/hosts
  - ☐ Activities

- ☐ Invite speaker(s)
    - ☐ Inform them about the event
    - ☐ Provide date, time, location
    - ☐ Request bio summary, photo, title of the presentation
    - ☐ Confirm equipment and AV needs
    - ☐ Note special requests (transportation, parking, food preference, etc.): _____
- ☐ Contact vendors & partners
    - ☐ Inform them about the event
    - ☐ Confirm availability, if they will be attending
    - ☐ Provide date, time, location
    - ☐ Request specific needs
    - ☐ Request logo, banners or other promotional pieces to use with event
- ☐ Identify mailing lists for target audiences
    - ☐ Addresses
    - ☐ Emails
- ☐ Identify specific media sources to target
    - ☐ Magazines, newspapers, radio, television, etc.
- ☐ Create a schedule for promotion of the event
    - ☐ Save-the-date
    - ☐ Invitation
    - ☐ eNewsletter
    - ☐ Press release(s)
    - ☐ Ads
    - ☐ Website: event page
    - ☐ Social media integration

Change. Adapt. Rock.
WildRock Public Relations & Marketing®

- [ ] On-site promotion
- [ ] Internal promotion to staff
- [ ] Design first drafts of promotional pieces: save-the-date, invitations, posters, ads, etc.
    - [ ] Develop a design theme and corresponding graphics
        - Considerations should include purposes of individual pieces: who will receive them, tone to be conveyed, how they will be produced and cost
    - [ ] Include all event details: date, time, location, program, specials, RSVP details

6-8 Weeks Before the Event

- [ ] Finalize event outline and layout
    - [ ] Location space and room set-ups
    - [ ] Menus and other catering services
    - [ ] Equipment, AV and supplies needed
- [ ] Finalize invitation list and mailing lists
- [ ] Identify VIP guests
- [ ] Addresses
- [ ] Emails
- [ ] Order printed materials and signage (may need to be done earlier depending on schedule set)
    - [ ] Invitations
    - [ ] Promotional pieces: posters, flyers, coupons, menus, postcards, etc.
    - [ ] Registration signage
    - [ ] Directional signage
    - [ ] Tickets (if for a nonprofit event, remember to list the value of goods and services received)
- [ ] Order gifts and/or other promotional items

4-6 Weeks Before the Event

- [ ] Mail invitations
    - [ ] Include suggested attire, RSVP date and other important event details
- [ ] Heavily promote the event across all identified channels
    - [ ] Include event invitation in eNewsletter
    - [ ] Place promotional pieces on site: posters, flyers, etc.
    - [ ] Website
    - [ ] Social media integration
    - [ ] Internal communications
    - [ ] Media placement: ads
    - [ ] Media pitches
    - [ ] Event calendar submissions

2 Weeks Before the Event

- [ ] Follow up on event promotion efforts
- [ ] Monitor RSVPs with regular reports
- [ ] Create and maintain a waiting list if event seating is limited
- [ ] Send email reminders
- [ ] Create event set-up and tear-down checklists
- [ ] Confirm staff assignments
    - [ ] Communicate attire expectations
    - [ ] Assign duties before, during and after the event
- [ ] Assign hosts for speakers and/or VIP guests

The Day of the Event

- [ ] Complete set-up
    - [ ] Check the function space at least one hour in advance to ensure set-up is complete

Visit www.wildrockpr.com/ready-to-rock or contact us at readytorock@wildrockpr.com for your FREE printable templates, checklists and forms to take notes as you read.

Change. Adapt. Rock.
WildRock Public Relations & Marketing®

- [ ] Complete tear-down
- [ ] Provide payment to vendors (if applicable)

Event Follow Up

- [ ] Send thank you cards to appropriate vendors, partners and speakers
- [ ] Create final attendance list
  - [ ] Include updated contact information for files
- [ ] Collect photos
  - [ ] Post on the website, include with eNewsletter and integrate into social media
- [ ] Compile event evaluation survey results (if applicable)
- [ ] Recap budget
  - [ ] Complete any outstanding payments
  - [ ] Update budget to reflect final event cost
  - [ ] Analyze cost per attendee
- [ ] Complete event evaluation
  - [ ] Program, presentation, speaker, food/beverage, gifts, venue, entertainment, etc.
  - [ ] Identify what went right, what could be done better, etc.
  - [ ] Determine if goals were achieved. If not, why?
  - [ ] This feedback should be documented for future planning usage

Who Do You Know?

You've probably heard the saying, "It's not what you know, it's who you know." Here's a fun exercise to get your network list going and have them join in on more of a grassroots PR scale. Your goal is to create a list of 100 people!

To start: go through your contacts on your phone, work and personal email to spark some ideas. Then, take it a step further by listing out:

- Friends/relatives/partner/spouse who supports your company?
- Worked with you at a former job?
- Former boss or supervisor?
- Is connected to you on social media (LinkedIn, Facebook, Instagram, Twitter, etc.)?
- People you regularly network with?
- People in your neighborhood?
- Former neighbor?
- Sat on a board/committee with?
- Owns a business?
- Has a family/friend who owns a business?
- Goes to your church?
- Goes to your gym?
- Your invite list for your wedding/major event/celebration/kid's birthday party?
- You went to high school or college with?
- Past teachers/professors?
- Met at a networking event?
- Professional service provider? (car dealer; barber/hairstylist; real estate agent; doctor or pediatrician; dentist; insurance agent; accountant/CPA; massage therapist; chiropractor; dermatologist; fitness instructor; lawyer; banker; minister; etc.)
- Someone you play sports with?
- If applicable, your children's friend's parents?
- People involved in your clubs?

Visit www.wildrockpr.com/ready-to-rock or contact us at readytorock@wildrockpr.com for your FREE printable templates, checklists and forms to take notes as you read.

Change. Adapt. Rock.
WildRock Public Relations & Marketing®

DIGITAL MARKETING
dig·i·tal mar·ket·ing | noun

Welcome to the party on the world wide web.

Much of life is online these days, and in order to go where people are, you need to build your brand there as well. Typically, when someone is researching a new product or service, online is the first place they go for information, companies and reviews. If you're not listed in those search results or don't provide adequate information, customers will go elsewhere to make a purchase.

Digital marketing is all about promoting your business using social media ads, search engine ads, search engine optimization (SEO), email marketing and more to reach new and existing customers through digital platforms. Compared to traditional marketing channels, it's low-cost and highly effective because it is measurable. By looking at how your digital marketing channels are performing, you'll be able to find out quickly whether your investment is working or if you need to try a different approach.

Digital marketing, and social media in particular, also allows for instant customer feedback. This can sometimes be considered a drawback as it requires you to be able to quickly respond, but if you can answer questions and concerns effectively, it can position your brand favorably in the long run.

A common misconception that we come across is that personal use of digital marketing platforms (especially social media) translates easily into being able to use these same platforms for business in a similar way. This is not the case.

Below you'll find cost-effective ways to get your business in the digital marketing game. To keep up, you need a foundational knowledge of marketing, paired with judgment to think critically, act independently and be fiercely creative as trends consistently evolve.

Digital marketing offers a variety of ways to grow your business. While it is known largely for its advertising opportunities, underneath that is a deeper focus on the customer by cultivating personal connections and building your marketing strategy around them. To do this, you must:

(1) Have a deep understanding of your customer, their demographics, online behaviors and purchasing preferences.

(2) Once you understand your customer, you can tailor your marketing approaches and target your audience.

(3) This, in turn, encourages customer loyalty and eventually brand advocacy.

There is also an amazing opportunity with digital marketing to tell the story behind your business.

 Storytelling through online content promotes the human components of your brand and fosters deeper relationships. It encourages customer engagement through relatable experiences and establishes approachability.

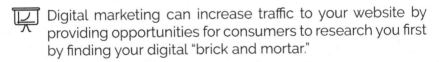 Digital marketing can increase traffic to your website by providing opportunities for consumers to research you first by finding your digital "brick and mortar."

You can then optimize your conversion rate, by evaluating through backend analytics, to see what makes customers engage with your brand online or where potential customers drop off. Understanding which approaches are successful and why they are working is crucial for launching data-driven business strategies for the future.

Ultimately, improving your story online will help you get discovered by boosting your search rankings to increase your audience and help provide data to determine your framework for long-term growth. To build your brand story, write out your customer problem, how you solve it and the successes your brand offers. This should only take two to three paragraphs. Make sure it captures the "why" behind your business and connects to your customers in a meaningful way. Once you have this, share it across multiple online platforms including your website and social media channels.

Chances are, you are already doing some form of digital marketing. However, some approaches might be more familiar than others. Below is a list of the most common types of digital marketing and some options for you to consider.

Explore Your Options

Most digital marketing works cohesively and if you start with a handful of tactics, you can add more over time. Below we have listed the main digital marketing tactics in order of most important (and with a level of difficulty rating: 1 easy, 2 somewhat hard and 3 advanced). See full definitions at the end of the book under Marketing Defined.

 Directory listing. Often the first place a potential customer will discover your business. This is a great place to start.

Level of difficulty = ▪▫▫

(2) Content marketing. Focuses on creating and distributing valuable and relevant content for a specific audience, it is not promotional content.

Level of difficulty = ▪▫▫

(3) Email marketing. Promotes products or services while building a relationship and encouraging brand interaction through email. Many programs have pre-developed templates you can use, but you will need powerful content to drive action.

Level of difficulty = ▪▪▫

(4) Chatbots and messenger. A new trend in communication providing information via messenger apps that promote a personalized experience and build trust with customers.

Level of difficulty = ▪▪▫

(5) Social media advertising. Attract traffic and attention using social media platforms by increasing exposure and building relationships with customers. This might include ads on Facebook, Instagram, Pinterest, Twitter or LinkedIn.

Level of difficulty = ▪▪▪

(6) Search engine optimization. Acquire quality traffic from organic search results by enhancing content for search engines and proliferating relevant traffic that will grow over time.

Level of difficulty = ▪▪▪

(7) Search engine marketing (SEM). Increase visibility in web searches through paid methods.

Level of difficulty = ▪▪▪

(8) Pay-per-click advertising (PPC). Purchase visits to your website and pay a fee every time someone clicks on your ads.

Level of difficulty = ▪▪▪

Foundations of Digital Marketing

Let's break down the foundations of digital marketing and highlight each portion to give you a deeper dive. We have also outlined some of our tried and true Rockstar Tips that even the novice marketer can execute. You've got this!

Directory Listings

Directory listings should always be up to date. Not only is local search on the rise, but this is also most likely the first place customers will look when wanting to contact you, both via web and phone. Keep in mind, there are numerous platforms such as Google (google.com), Yelp (yelp.com), TripAdvisor (tripadvisor.com) and more that your company may be listed on.

Creating online directory listings isn't hard but you do have to have some materials prepared in advance, follow the steps outlined in each platform, be prepared to follow up and, most importantly, be patient. Getting online directory listings is not an overnight process but they are well worth it (and free). Plus, once established, keeping them updated throughout the year only takes a few minutes.

Getting Started with Directory Listings

If you've never done directory listings, here is what you need to prepare in advance:

(1) Five to 10 high-resolution (300 dpi) images that are preferably lifestyle-themed but can include photos of your business interior and exterior.

(2) Company name, address, phone, website, brief company description (one to two sentences) and a logo.

(3) Email address and password to be used for account creation. Note: Google requires the use of a Gmail email. If you don't have one, create one first.

(4) Most setup processes use email verification, but some require a phone call. When you go to set up the accounts, make sure it's a time where you can answer the phone or check your inbox so you can complete the account creation. Note: The call will go to the business phone number tied to the listing, not your personal number.

(5) With Google, in particular, you'll need to select both primary and secondary categories.

(6) When setting up a new listing, Google verifies the account by mailing a postcard with a verification code to the address on the listing. Note: This can take seven to 12 business days and it expires after 30 days, so set reminders for yourself. Once the code is received, login and add it to the account profile.

Rockstar Tips for Growing Directory Listings

If you already have directory listings in place, here are some ways you can expand:

- Add more content; search engines love it! Update or expand company description, include seasonal updates and add new photos.

- Always make sure your hours of operation and contact information (such as address and phone number) are up to date. If your business changes seasonally, make sure to update the description and photos to reflect it.

- Set reoccurring calendar reminders quarterly to update the listings and make any necessary changes. It's a good idea to update photos as well, especially for changing seasons.

Rockstar Tips for Growing Directory Listings

- Respond to comments and reviews ASAP, both positive and negative, as this impacts your search results. If it's negative, briefly take accountability and offer to right the solution immediately. Encourage the reviewer to contact you directly so you can take the conversation offline.

  - Note: if it's a bad review, you cannot remove it. However, Google does allow you to flag fake reviews and Facebook allows you to either turn off reviews or report false ones.

- Share positive reviews on social media.

- Too many listings? Consider a program like Yext (yext.com) to manage all of your options with one global update.

This is an example of a Rockstar review on Facebook.

Ice Pirates Backcountry Adventures Snowmobile Tours
Published by Sprout Social [?] · April 22 · 🌐

"My wife and I were visiting Durango on Feb 17, 2020, and we scheduled a private tour with James. IT WAS AMAZING AND THE MOST FUN DAY OF OUR TRIP. Our guide was knowledgable, friendly, and very fun to be with during the day. The equipment we were on was brand new, in great shape and easy to get used to. We would definitely recommend Ice Pirates for your snowmobile adventure and James as your guide. and Terri, Indianapolis, IN 😊" -Joe

205
People Reached

👍 14

14
Engagements

👍 Like   💬 Comment   ↪ Share   Boost Post

Comment as Ice Pirates Backcountry Adventure...

Content Marketing

Content marketing pulls together some of the things you do for strong SEO but looks at how to deliver those pieces to a larger audience and grow your website traffic at the same time. Content marketing includes articles, blogs, case studies, infographics, videos, whitepapers and more in areas of your industry where you can be the expert. See more in our content section.

 Rockstar Tips for Content Marketing

- Use what you have. Update and repurpose previously created content by making sure it is still relevant. You can do this by making the content align with the season or sales cycle and adding new keywords or repurposing text into another format like a video. When you repost the content, make sure to add a new date.

- Don't have a lot of old content to repurpose? Create new content! Review your target audience first to determine what content will best resonate. Then, outline the main topics for your content along with supporting details. After that, you can begin writing.

- Not sure which topic to begin with? What are the top questions people have about your service or product? Answer those.

- Length can vary depending on the content. Ideal lengths for headlines are six words; about 500 words for a case study; 1,500 words for a blog post and eight to 10 pages for a whitepaper. Videos, on the other hand, should be one minute or less.

- Ideally, you should be creating new content or repurposing old content every month.

- Once it's created, share it everywhere. Utilize multiple digital channels to post your content. For example, if you post a new blog, share the links on social media channels and email newsletters and be consistent in your messaging across platforms.

Email Marketing

Email marketing is essential for keeping your current customer base engaged, along with reaching and nurturing new users. Simply put, email marketing is when businesses use email programs to promote their product or service to subscribers. Even if you have never done email marketing before, there are helpful, easy-to-use products like MailChimp (mailchimp. com) (free under 2,000 subscribers) and Constant Contact (constantcontact.com) (fee-based, free 60-day trial) that you can use to help build your emails and grow your audience. We recommend using a professional email program so you can comply with CAN-SPAM laws, which include having a one-click email opt-out within the email. Visit the FTC (ftc.gov) website and see our definitions section for more information.

Getting Started with Email Marketing

Similar to directory listings, if you've never done email marketing, here is what you need to prepare in advance:

(1) Company name, address, phone, website, brief company description (one to two sentences), contact information and logo.

(2) Email address and password to be used for account creation. Note: We recommend using an "info@" email address when possible for the email setup and contact information.

(3) Contact list, typically in an Excel or CSV format, with email in the first column and first name in the second column. Note: Some email programs, like MailChimp, remove duplicate emails from the list. If not, make sure to do this before your first send.

Change. Adapt. Rock.
WildRock Public Relations & Marketing®

(4) With the design, you want to figure out what kind of content you'll be emailing regularly. That will help determine what template you select. If you already have an email program, you can duplicate the campaign and edit the design, or create a new design and use it as a template moving forward. Note: Always be sure to choose a template that is mobile responsive to create a better user experience on all devices.

(5) Content, including text, images and links, should also be developed in advance so all you have to do is copy and paste directly into your template.

Rockstar Tips for Email Marketing

- Develop a segmented email audience list. Perhaps some people on your list are just general business connections and others might be customers. Maybe you separate your list by state or demographic. Think about the information you will email out and how that might be received by each audience. You have your own preferences and so do your contacts.

- Most emails are skimmed. Keep your content simple by not loading your email communications with too many updates for users to read. Focus on one new item and one product/ service with a description between 100 to 200 words. Strong visuals can also be helpful to convey your message quickly.

- Subject lines, like a headline, should also be short and sweet. Aim to write somewhere between 28 to 50 characters for the subject line.

Rockstar Tips for Email Marketing

- Find a good cadence when sending emails. Don't just send one when the mood strikes. Create a six-month schedule with monthly, bi-monthly or weekly emails. Try not to send emails more than once a week. Your customers will get conditioned to expect them in their inbox and it will allow you to be more thoughtful and intentional with content. Plus, you'll know if you're sending too many when your opens and click-throughs steadily decline. At that point, consider a list scrub (removing people from your list who aren't active on your email list) and allow only interested subscribers to resubscribe.

- There are many ways to build your email list. You can add an email signup form, or an email list pop-up, on your website for exclusive content or promotion. You can request email addresses as part of a social media promotion, contest or ad campaign. You can even use events, networking opportunities and webinars as tools to collect email signups.

- Hubspot (hubspot.com) has some great examples of stellar email campaigns.

Polaris Adventures ✓
November 12, 2019 · 🌐

We've partnered with GoWild for the Build Your Adventure Sweepstakes. Download the GoWild app with the link below and vote for one of five epic adventures you would most like to experience! The location with the top votes will be given away to one lucky member!
http://mygowild.com/PolarisAdventures_GoWild

🖒 Like Page

GoWild
November 10, 2019 · 🌐

We've partnered with Polaris Adventures for the Build Your Adventure Sweepstakes. Download the GoWild app with the link below and vote for one of five epic adventures you would most like to experience! The location with the top votes will be given away to one lucky member!
http://mygowild.com/PolarisAdventures_GoWild

52
Engagements

Boost Unavailable

1,102
People Reached

3 Shares

🖒 18

🖒 Like   💬 Comment   ↪ Share

This is an example of a Rockstar sweepstakes Polaris Adventures ran in partnership with GoWild that included an all-expense-paid trip to an epic location. A creative and effective way to build an email database!

Change. Adapt. Rock.
WildRock Public Relations & Marketing®

Chatbot and Messenger Marketing

Chatbot and messenger marketing can be extremely complex with questions, dialogue flow and mapping. Many agencies create these flows to make it feel like you are having a true artificial intelligence (AI) experience. But there are some beginner ways to take advantage of this technology that can help your business.

Getting Started with Chatbot and Messenger Marketing for Facebook

If you've never engaged in chatbot or messenger marketing, here are some tips to help you get started:

1. Go to the Facebook section of Creator Studio.

2. Select your inbox and turn on "Automatic Responses."

3. Click the edit messages button to start your journey in chat automation.

4. Set these four easy messenger automations: away message, instant reply, contact information request and location request.

Growing Chatbot and Messenger Marketing

If you already have basic chatbot or messenger marketing in place, here are some ways you can expand:

1. Look for a low-cost or free chat builder tool like Chatfuel (chatfuel.com) or Manychat (manychat.com).

2. These sites have basic templates that are already created so you can skip the frustration.

Rockstar Tips for Chatbot & Messenger Marketing

- Develop a common list of questions you currently answer often via email or messenger.

- Check out Facebook Messenger (messenger.com) for major brands, like Pizza Hut, to get ideas of what messenger bots look like for them. Check out chatbotguide.org for best practices and examples of how major brands are using chatbots.

- Add your basic information to be accessed from these automated messenger systems. Think of things to add like your hours of operations or simple messages letting customers know you will be back with them soon.

- Create a resource with FAQ questions to be automatically answered to help cut down on emails and phone calls. Some items to cover might be directly related to products and services and may already exist on your website but add them here as well.

Social Media Advertising

Social media advertising seems like the easiest place to start your digital marketing efforts, but the complexity of proper testing and targeting can lead to frustration and quickly waste time, and more importantly, money. We recommend starting small, picking one or two platforms you think would resonate with your target audience or maybe a platform you're already using successfully. Start with a couple of ads and a smaller spend such as $100, then try and test.

Try different headlines, copy, creative or all of the ad's visual attributes and audience combinations. Once you have data for what's working and what's not, then expand upon what works. Try more ads, expand to more audiences and increase your spending. When you're feeling more confident, expand to other platforms. Don't forget to test again as every platform takes a different approach and requires a different message.

Getting Started with Social Media Advertising – Facebook and Instagram

If you've never done social media advertising, here are some tips to help you get started:

(1) For Facebook/Instagram, locate the Ad Account setup under Settings.

(2) Set up an Ad Account with credit card information, time zone and currency.

(3) For legal purposes, you'll also need to answer questions as to why you're setting up an ad account. This includes basic business information such as name, address, country and tax ID number.

(4) If you want to advertise on Instagram at the same time, link your Facebook and Instagram accounts under Settings, Instagram.

(5) You'll also want to determine your advertising objective. Choose from awareness, consideration or conversion. The most common is to increase traffic and engagement through a consideration objective or reach through an awareness objective.

(6) Next, set up the audience targeting. This includes location, age, gender, language, detailed targeting and connections. Detailed targeting can help you refine an audience with interest and behaviors such as business, family composition, hobbies, fitness, shopping, sports, technology and more. Save your audience targeting details for future use as well.

(7) Unless you've done testing or are launching a mobile-only campaign, we recommend you select automatic placement.

(8) From there, set up a budget and bidding. We recommend starting in the middle of the range for bids and adjusting from there.

Getting Started with Social Media Advertising – LinkedIn

(1) For LinkedIn, you can find the ad setup under Campaign Manager (linkedin.com/campaignmanager).

(2) Similar to Facebook, you'll want to select a campaign objective that fits your goals: awareness, consideration or conversions.

(3) From there, you will build your target audience, including location, company, job experience, education, interests and demographics.

(4) After that, you'll select your ad format. Choose a sponsored post (single image, carousel or video ads), message ad (InMail) or text ads.

(5) Then, set your bid and budget.

Growing Social Media Advertising

If you already have baseline social media advertising in place, here are some ways you can expand:

(1) As we mentioned previously, testing, also called A/B split testing, is the prime way to learn what's working and what's not when it comes to ad campaigns. Both Facebook (facebook.com) and Google (google.com) offer platforms conducive to testing and optimization.

(2) Revisit your campaign objective and make sure it's the right one for your goals.

(3) Optimize your ads by only running them on the days and hours during the week when they perform well. You can do this by selecting Run Ads on a schedule under Ad Scheduling. For example, you may choose to turn things off over the weekend.

(4) Switch out ad design, including images and ad copy, so your ad doesn't become too repetitive and easily ignored.

(5) Dial-in your ad placement on Facebook and Google by reviewing how your ad performed in various placements and increase your budget on the top ones.

Rockstar Tips for Social Media Advertising

- Compelling imagery and concise, punchy copy are basic recipes for ad success.

- Select a channel that has demographics that match your brand. Sprout Social (sproutsocial.com), a social media scheduling and monitoring platform provides great insight into demographics by each social media channel.

- LinkedIn has compiled a fast data port of business professionals that is perfectly suited for business to business (B2B) marketing. Look to keep your marketing simple with boosted posts using basic geography targeting.

- Facebook and Instagram ads can be set up and managed from the same platform, which makes it a great option for business-to-consumer (B2C) brands. You can even run the same ad across both platforms in different placements automatically. With a wide variety of campaign objectives, you can optimize for everything from brand awareness to conversions.

- Twitter allows you to promote tweets or entire campaigns to expand your existing reach on the platform. Since people scroll through the platform quickly, you'll need to make sure your ad gets to the point fast.

Rockstar Tips for Social Media Advertising

- Pinterest (pinterest.com) is a discovery platform and designed to promote product and gift ideas. Almost all searches on Pinterest are unbranded. You'll want to make sure you have an established and successful presence on Pinterest before you consider advertising. Make sure you have beautiful imagery and lead with a hook in your copy.

- While industry benchmarks can be helpful guidelines, ultimately you should use your own ad performance for baseline measurements and future goals.

Search Engine Optimization

SEO can sound like an extremely complicated part of the digital footprint; however, basic concepts are easy to grasp and can make a big difference in your business! Without SEO you may very well be SOL so let's get started!

Basic SEO is free (we love that word) and can make a huge impact in getting your content and website ranking higher on search engines. So, why is a good ranking so important?

Rankings help customers find you instead of your competitors when they are searching for keywords related to your business. It also helps drive qualified traffic to your site, because people find the exact product or service they want. The stronger your SEO strategy, the more likely your website will pop up in your target audiences' online searches.

Search Engine Optimization

SEO can sound like an extremely complicated part of the digital footprint; however, basic concepts are easy to grasp and can make a big difference in your business! Without SEO you may very well be SOL so let's get started!

Basic SEO is free (we love that word) and can make a huge impact in getting your content and website ranking higher on search engines. So, why is a good ranking so important?

Rankings help customers find you instead of your competitors when they are searching for keywords related to your business. It also helps drive qualified traffic to your site, because people find the exact product or service they want. The stronger your SEO strategy, the more likely your website will pop up in your target audiences' online searches.

<u>Getting Started with SEO</u>

If you've never done SEO, here are some tips to help you get started:

- Type in some keywords that you think are being used to find your business. See how well your website ranks in search engines.
- Review your website analytics (most often Google Analytics) to uncover:
    - Audience Overview to understand your website traffic.
    - Audience Geo so you know where your traffic lives.
    - Behavior Overview for top pages so you know where your website traffic is going.
    - Behavior, Site Content, Exit Pages so you know where your website traffic is exiting.
    - Acquisition, All Traffic, Referrals so you know what sites are driving traffic to yours.

- Make sure your website has an SEO plugin like Yoast (yoast.com) or All In One SEO Pack. If your site doesn't have one, or if you're not comfortable installing it, contact a website developer for help.
  - If you do have an SEO plugin but have never used one before, there are some great video tutorials online that we recommend you watch first as this technology is always changing.
- List descriptions of your products, services, target markets and target locations. These are not embellished, but rather straightforward descriptions. You will use these later.
- Identify your keywords through a tool such as Ahrefs (ahrefs.com), SEMRush (semrush.com) or Google Keyword Planner. Some of these require paid subscriptions or account set up to use, but, oftentimes, you can use them for a solid keywords list on a free trial basis.
- Once you've identified your keywords, make sure they are added to the product and/or service descriptions above along with target locations.
- You are now ready to create your SEO content, called tags. This includes title, meta description and keyword. We recommend drafting these in a Word document in advance. Ideally, character length for titles is 50 to 60 and can go up to 120 characters for meta descriptions. Ahrefs provides a good breakdown of tags, what they are and how they are important to SEO.
- Once complete, they can be added directly to every page on your website via the plugin, such as Yoast.

NEED HELP WITH SEO?

WildRock's Rockstars are here to help solve your biggest digital marketing challenges. Learn more at www.wildrockpr.com.

Growing SEO

If you already have baseline SEO in place, here are some ways you can optimize your efforts:

(1) Identify one main keyword or phrase you want to optimize per web page.

(2) Make sure that keyword is in the title, meta description and the actual page content that viewers see.

(3) Use one of the keyword tools mentioned previously to find similar or related phrases to your main keywords that may help you scoop up more valuable traffic. Add these phrases into your website content.

(4) Refresh and expand your existing content on your website. One thing we often see with new or small businesses is very little text on websites, which results in poor website search rankings.

(5) Add relevant links to your website content, where appropriate. Both external links and links within your website are useful. Links tell search engines that your content is important and helps improve search results, but make sure you only link to a legitimate site.

Here's a checklist of pro tips to ensure your SEO rocks

☐ Content is key. Create unique content in the form of blogs, listicles, articles and how-tos monthly. The key is having unique content that you create, specifically related to your business service or product. Even better, weave in a keyword or two.

☐ Create a 1,000-word article or freshen up an existing blog every quarter. Writing that much about your services and products can seem hard, but if you get into the specific details and highlight advantages to your target audiences, you can push the length of your content. You can write it in phases, try 200 words a day!

☐ Front-load keywords into the beginning of your page titles and make sure that the keyword is in the first 100 to 150 words on the page.

☐ Use one H1 on every page of your website and include your keywords in it. An H1 is the first header visible on your web page and the most important header from a search perspective.

☐ Fill in the "alt" tags on your website's images. Alt tags are alternative text for your website's photos and images that speak specifically to search engines. You can usually access this on the back end of your website by clicking on the image itself or through the media library.

☐ Finally, check your progress. Remember when you typed in keywords that were being used to find your business at the beginning of this process? Do it again to see how much your search rankings have improved. You can also use the keyword tools above to see how well your site is ranking on your main keywords.

Visit www.wildrockpr.com/ready-to-rock or contact us at readytorock@wildrockpr.com for your FREE printable templates, checklists and forms to take notes as you read.

Change. Adapt. Rock.
WildRock Public Relations & Marketing®

Search Engine Marketing

Search engine marketing is the key to appear at the top of your favorite search engine, typically Google, through keyword searches. Putting your product or service at the top of the search result page will virtually guarantee clicks directly to your website. This is a type of Pay Per Click (PPC) channel, but dollars alone won't get you those clicks. You will still need to develop catchy headlines and content.

Getting Started with SEM

If you've never done SEM, here are some tips to help you get started:

(1) Set up a Google Ads account (ads.google.com). If you're not sure how there are a lot of great tutorials online that can walk you through this step-by-step.

(2) If you already have a Google Analytics account, link your new Ads account to it under Settings.

(3) If you haven't already, perform keyword research. You will use these keywords in your ad copy as well as in your ad campaign setup.

(4) Write down your ad goals; target audience; main product or service you want to promote; your budget or how much you want to spend; as well as a timeline for the campaign.

(5) Now you are ready to write your search ad. All headlines (three total) are 30 characters, all descriptions (two total) are 90 characters and all URLs (two total) are 15 characters. Headlines should be catchy and descriptions should be useful with a clear call to action (CTA).

6 Once you have your search ad copy, you are ready to create a campaign in Google Ads. If you're not sure how, there are a lot of great tutorials online that can walk you through this step-by-step. PPC Protect provides some great examples of awesome Google Ads.

Growing SEM

If you already have baseline SEM in place, here are some ways you can expand:

1 Take your audience targeting a layer deeper by reviewing habits and interests under affinity, detailed demographics and intent to purchase under in-market.

2 Refine your target locations so you're only spending budget on geo-locations that are responsive to your ad.

3 Run a remarketing campaign to target users who have already shown interest by visiting your website.

4 Review your keyword performance and eliminate poorly performing keywords so you can just focus your ad budget on what's working.

5 Review your clicks, impressions and click-through rates as the key statistics to know if your ads are successful.

6 Google also offers keyword recommendations. This allows you to add relevant keywords to your ad even while it's running to help scoop up more traffic.

Rockstar Tips for SEM

- Pick one search engine. Google is still the top browser as far as search engines go. Start here with simple search advertising.

- Strengthen your ad strategy by pairing your search ads with other forms of advertising like social media.

- Create an eye-catching headline, such as, "Your Next Adventure Awaits." This may start with some competitor research to see what others in the industry are using in their search ads. Don't copy their headlines but use them to find ways to make yours stand out and show your value proposition.

- There are lots of tools to see what ads your competitors are running, such as Spyfu and Moat. To use these tools, you will need to create an account and have your competitor's URLs listed. Once you add the URLs, the program brings up the keywords and ad copy of your competitors. Voilà!

- You will know your ad is working when you start getting more website traffic and that traffic is converting by buying your product or service. If your brand is relatively unknown, it can sometimes take up to three months to develop brand awareness among your target audience.

PPC or Display Advertising

PPC, or display advertising, can be very advantageous for some brands. But this is another area where you get into more advanced practices that usually require a dedicated and expert resource. The combination of stunning creative, or visual attributes, along with targeting and retargeting objectives is something you should leave to the pros. If you've already gotten started with PPC and you're looking to elevate your efforts, check out our Rockstar Tips!

Growing Your PPC Program

If you already have baseline PPC in place and you are familiar with the platforms, here are some ways you can expand:

(1) Try a remarketing campaign that shows ads to people who have already visited your website.

(2) Take your targeting a layer deeper with managed placements that allow you to choose the exact sites your ads are displayed on. Not sure where to start? Look at your referral traffic in Google Analytics to see what websites are driving traffic to your site.

(3) Similarly, you can also exclude underperforming placements. Review your placement lists and make sure they are showing up on sites that are relevant to your product or audience.

(4) Ads should always be simple, visual and easy to read. Remember you only have a few seconds to catch the attention of your audience and get a click.

(5) Use a free and easy program to create your ads. We recommend Canva to make your ads visually stunning.

Rockstar Tips for PPC

- Simplify your targeting to location and keywords. Other advanced methods like retargeting and detailed targeting can be valuable but require a learning curve.
- Size does matter. Be sure to include the most popular Google display ad sizes for both mobile and desktop.

Rockstar Tips for PPC

Mobile Ads in pixels
- 300 x 250
- 320 x 100
- 250 x 250 – Square
- 200 x 200 – Small Square

Desktop Ads in pixels
- 300 x 250
- 336 x 280 – Large Rectangle
- 728 x 90 – Leaderboard
- 300 x 600 – Half-Page Ad
- 160 x 600 – Wide Skyscraper
- 970 x 90 – Large Leaderboard
- 468 x 60 – Banner
- 250 x 250 – Square
- 200 x 200 – Small Square

Perhaps you're just dabbling with the idea of incorporating some of these approaches into your marketing strategy. Maybe you've mastered a few forms of digital marketing but want to explore more. We've studied the ins and outs of digital marketing, and we know how important it is to navigate your strategies to uniquely benefit your company. There are so many different approaches to digital marketing, so one size does not fit all.

Ready to launch a new campaign? We've provided some helpful reminders and a checklist for your launch.

Digital Marketing Ideas

Because digital marketing changes rapidly, we encourage you to research further to ensure channels still have the same requirements.

- **Encourage a higher conversion by engaging in social commerce and shoppable posts.** Reduce the risk of customers abandoning their purchase to switch apps or sign-in to an unknown store by enabling them to shop directly in a social media platform. Shopify (shopify.com) is one of the most popular platforms to utilize.

- **Leverage smart bidding in Google Ads.** Utilize artificial intelligence to optimize the number of conversions or conversion value at each auction (also known as "auction-time bidding").

- **Consider Augmented Reality (AR).** Enhance and modernize the customer experience through computerized "try before you buy," which can subsequently provide business opportunities and boost sales.

- **Create a discount or promotion.** When used effectively, an online discount can drive customer loyalty, move inventory and increase conversions. The most common discounts are percentage off, dollar amount off, free shipping or a free gift with an automatic discount that applies to all eligible shopping carts or through a discount code. When promoting the discount, make sure you clearly state the date range for when the discount can be applied and any exclusions.

Rockstar Tips for Digital Marketing

- Use discounts to launch new products, seasonal sales (like the holidays), abandon cart offers, email sign up offer, first-time shopper, minimum purchase, customer loyalty offer and customer milestone discount. Shopify offers some perspective on how to best use discounts.

- Google, Facebook, Instagram, LinkedIn and other digital advertising platforms work together to play a key role in a customer's buying progression. Some brands like Sephora have taken that a step further with shoppable content on platforms like Instagram.

- Efforts should include similar graphics, messaging and calls to action.

- Creative and messaging should be customized for each audience you are trying to reach.

Digital Marketing Checklists

Pre-Launch Checklist

- [ ] What are your campaign goals?
- [ ] Who is your target audience?
  - [ ] Are there custom audience, lookalike or retargeting options available?
  - [ ] Do you know their age, gender, location(s), interests, etc.?
  - [ ] What are their purchasing preferences?
  - [ ] What are their online behaviors?

☐ What does success look like?

☐ How will you measure success (for example, page growth, post engagement, website clicks or sales)?

☐ Determine the total digital ad budget.

☐ What are your key messages?

☐ Do you have a clear and compelling call to action (CTA)?

☐ What will your creative look like?

☐ Does your creative meet the channel text and design requirements? Resolution by pixels is listed below.

   ☐ Facebook and Instagram: 1,080 x 1,080 pixels. Only 20% of your ad can contain text. You can use the Text Overlay tool to check your ad in advance.

   ☐ Google Display varies, typical sizes include 250 x 250 pixels for square, 240 x 400 pixels for vertical rectangle, 120 x 600 pixels for skyscraper, 468 x 60 pixels for banner and 728 x 90 pixels for leaderboard.

☐ Will you do A/B testing to see what works (for example, testing different audiences, images, copy, headlines, CTAs, types of ads, etc.)?

Post-Launch Checklist

☐ Is your creative working? Monitor ads daily, especially in the beginning, and make adjustments to improve results.

☐ Ensure that comments are appropriate and are frequently managed.

☐ Keep Facebook ad frequency rates below three.

☐ Compare cost-per-click results to industry averages.

☐ Review ads for delayed or slow delivery.

Visit www.wildrockpr.com/ready-to-rock or contact us at readytorock@wildrockpr.com for your FREE printable templates, checklists and forms to take notes as you read.

Change. Adapt. Rock.
WildRock Public Relations & Marketing®

CONTENT
con·tent | noun

Words collected together to paint a beautiful picture of your business.

Don't be content with lame content. With millions of eyes online, content is key - make sure your message stands out from the crowd. Digital communication is crucial and presents a chance to strengthen the connection with your audience and improve your brand image.

How do you create unique content that stands out without getting lost in the sea of subpar? It's important to be mindful of your message. Posting in the right place, posting at the right time, targeting the appropriate audience and telling your authentic story will keep you ahead of the curve.

To create good content, think of your brand as a story that needs to be told. Include history, challenges, successes, milestones and what makes you unique. Ultimately, you want to make your brand relatable and connect with people to evoke an emotional response in your customers.

Remember, the content that you create can tell a visual story about your brand. Pairing your words with the right image, graphic or video can make all the difference. If you don't have an asset library of visual media, there are dozens of free stock image and video sites you can use (see list on the following page). Due to copyright issues, don't be tempted to download and use protected images off the internet.

Free Stock Photo Sites

StockSnap.io
stocksnap.io

Pexels
pexels.com

Unsplash
unsplash.com

Burst
burst.shopify.com

Reshot
reshot.com

Pixabay
pixabay.com

FoodiesFeed
foodiesfeed.com

Freestocks.org
freestocks.org

Picography
picography.co

PicJumbo
picjumbo.com

ISO Republic
isorepublic.com

To decide which channels to use for your content, revisit your target audience(s). How do they like to receive information? Are you targeting Millennials who are active on social media or Baby Boomers who like to receive email newsletters? Make sure the content you create fits the channel and audience it's intended to reach.

Be aware of where people stand in relation to your business. Have they heard of you before? Are they considering buying or engaging? Or possibly they know you, love you and are already brand loyalists. This is important to consider so you can customize your content.

📝 Rockstar Tips for Content

- Focus on highlighting your customers' needs/wants and how you can help fulfill those needs.

- Stick with the platforms and channels where your current and/or desired customers are. Don't waste time and energy creating content for irrelevant or unsuccessful channels.

- Behind-the-scenes content, such as a social media post highlighting your team hard at work, is a great way to connect.

- Be part of the global conversation, but talk about what you know and your unique perspective.

- Instead of pitching your products or services, deliver information that helps inform your customers before they buy.

- Testimonials can be successful in catching customers' attention and relating to their wants and needs.

- Constantly creating useful content for your website or blog will make Google think that you are a lead player in the game, which gives you an advantage with search engines.

- Repurpose when and where you can; you don't need to recreate the wheel. For instance, longer forms of content, such as a blog, can be broken down into smaller social media posts.

- Keep track of what questions your audiences are repeatedly asking and create content to answer those questions.

- Show people why they need you, why you will make their lives easier and how you can help with their problems.

- Keep it simple. Don't make the content too long or complex. Simply state what you need to in a clear concise manner.

- Use correct grammar and spelling. Use programs like Grammarly to help proofread and ensure professional and polished content.

Map Out Your Content

Content in today's world needs to be unique and customized. Customers want their individual wants and needs heard. Content isn't "one-size-fits-all." Furthermore, even customers with similar characteristics will be at different levels of interaction with your business. Some customers may be just learning about you, while others may be more established and had previous interactions. Different messaging will resonate with different people, so make sure the content you're producing across your channels says all the right things about you.

In your strategy, you included your target audiences and key messages, now let's take that to the next level with a content mapping exercise. This exercise will help you understand what your customers need, plan your targeted messaging and know which channels to use.

Use the following template to get you started. You can have as many, or as few, personas as you like.

Change. Adapt. Rock.
WildRock Public Relations & Marketing®

Customer Persona 1	Lifecycle Stage			Preferred Communication Channels
Customer #1 Name: [Fill in the name of the customer. Get as specific as you want or need.]	**Awareness**	**Consideration**	**Decision**	[Fill in the best channels to reach Customer #1. For example, email, social media, blogs, etc.]
Wants, Needs, Problem/ Opportunity Customer #1 Needs Help With: [Fill in the core challenges, needs, goals, etc. for this customer to keep as a guide to map out your content.]	**Messaging** [Fill in content ideas, call to action (CTA), etc. for Customer #1 in the awareness stage.]	**Messaging** [Fill in content ideas, CTA, etc. for Customer #1 in the consideration stage.]	**Messaging** [Fill in content ideas, CTA, etc. for Customer #1 in the decision stage.]	

Once you have your content map completed, you can use it to guide your content creation across all of your channels. Keep this document handy and reference it often. Ensure everything in your emails, social content and blog posts addresses your customers' needs and sticks to your key messaging points.

Content in Times of Change

Change can be difficult. However, with these tools you can make it easier. You should constantly revise your content to make sure your message is relevant. This is especially important during times of change. We've created an additional list of Rockstar Tips to help guide you through content creation to stay relevant, while also sensitive, during a pandemic, recession or other significant time.

<u>Times of Change Content Checklist</u>

☐ Did I stay compassionate? Empathy is key for connecting with your audience.

☐ Did I stay positive? Use an optimistic and helpful tone to encourage people during challenging times.

☐ Did I avoid a humorous, sarcastic or casual feel? Content should be appropriate to prevent sounding unsympathetic.

☐ Was I mindful of insensitive words?

☐ Did I make any promises, guarantees or predictions? The future may change.

☐ Am I consistently adjusting for relevance? Content that has worked in the past may not be appropriate today. Make changes accordingly.

☐ Did I double-check previous messaging and posts? Check your scheduled content. Review automated posts and make edits as necessary.

Visit www.wildrockpr.com/ready-to-rock or contact us at readytorock@wildrockpr.com for your FREE printable templates, checklists and forms to take notes as you read.

Change. Adapt. Rock.
WildRock Public Relations & Marketing®

Rockstar Tips for Proofing

Proofing your work can be challenging when you've been in creation mode. Here are some tips so you can switch gears and transition smoothly into editing:

(1) Upload the document into Grammarly for a quick and easy spellcheck.

(2) Read the copy out loud.

(3) Read it slowly.

(4) Point with your finger and read one word at a time.

(5) Sleep on it and give it a fresh read in the morning.

(6) Print it out so you can edit it in a different format.

(7) Have someone else give it a read.

(8) Change the font size or font in general.

SOCIAL MEDIA
so·cial med·i·a | noun

Places where customers hang out just waiting to hear about your Rockstar business.

Social media can't be ignored when composing your strategy. It is a huge marketplace for business today. When it comes to social media, it is important to keep track of trends and changes.

 How are audiences responding on certain platforms?

 Which networks are seeing the most engagement?

 When is the best time to post?

 Keeping an eye on social networks and how they are affected can keep your business relevant and ahead of the pack.

Using your business goals from your PR and marketing strategy, map out how social media will support your objectives, then tie it to a metric. You can find social media metrics for your Facebook page, for example, under Insights. Each tab provides metrics for page performance.

Social Media Objectives

Use this template below to get started. We've filled in a few examples:

Business Objective	Social Media Goal	Metric
Grow the brand	Awareness and reaching new fans	Likes, followers
Drive leads and sales	Website clicks and conversions	Website clicks, email sign-ups, Shopify sales
Turn customers into advocates	Engagement	Comments, likes, @mentions

What to Post

So, where do you start? Whether your channels are new or have been up and running for awhile, make sure you define your content mix before you jump right to posting. Content is the fuel you'll use to engage with your audience, so you will want to make sure you're filled up and ready to go.

Here are a few standard content types to consider in your posts:

 Entertainment

 Inspiration

 Conversation starters

 How-to tutorials

 Education

Promotion (limit how many of these you post, keep it to one promotional post for every four education, inspiration, entertainment, etc. posts)

Do a quick exercise and spend 15 minutes thinking about each of these content types, your business and all the content you already have or could create. Write down anything that comes to mind and classify it into one of the categories above. This will get you started with some initial posts.

Rockstar Tips for What to Post & Being Creative

Sometimes it's hard to be creative on the spot. Here are some ideas to get your creative juices flowing:

- **Be authentic.** Content for social media should be engaging and true to your brand. Limit the amount of overly-promotional content you post or you may risk losing followers.

- **Create content that encourages engagement.** Utilize dynamic content that provides a more immersive experience by including trends like quizzes, polls, calculators, 360-degree videos, etc. in your social media content. A lot of platforms have these built-in, which makes them easy to use, i.e. the Instagram Story stickers.

- **Relationships first.** Organic social media is about relationships, so focus on engaging in conversations and building awareness, credibility and trust. By focusing on content that educates and entertains, you create a more welcoming environment for your audience, so they are more open to promotional messages when you do share them.

- **Request user-generated content (UGC).** Encourage audiences to share content by providing an incentive or joining with them for a good cause to improve engagement and drive conversion rates. Make sure you engage back with their content; you could even share their content to your channels.

- **Search.** Find inspiring news headlines to stimulate ideas (search keywords on the target audiences, product information, competitors, etc.). Search Google Images for pictures that describe the idea/concept you are trying to convey; this sometimes helps spark ideas.

Polaris Adventures
Published by Sprout Social [?] · May 13 at 1:26 PM · 🌐

Settle in for a virtual ride-along. Today we'll drive to the top of the New Hampshire mountains to take in this beautiful world. #keeponadventuring

884
People Reached

55
Engagements

Boost Post

👍❤️😮 29

👍 Like   💬 Comment   ↪ Share   1 Comment

This is an example of a Rockstar post. The image is crisp, not fuzzy. The copy is short, and compelling without being overly promotional. It also includes a relevant hashtag.

Rockstar Tips for What to Post & Being Creative

- **Change scenery.** Go to a coffee shop or work from home one afternoon.

- **Take a break.** Refresh your mind and go on a quick walk, run or catch a yoga class. Sometimes fresh air or a break helps to get the ideas going.

- **Ask a friend.** Bounce ideas around with your team or a friend and ask, "I'm playing with this concept. What do you think? Can we walk through this?"

- **Write first, edit later.** On your first draft, let your thoughts flow without editing or correcting yourself as you go. This will help you tap into your creativity. Once you've written out all of the ideas, then go back and edit and rearrange.

- **Shorten your sentences.** Keep it simple by putting your information in what we like to call "snackable bites" by explaining one idea per sentence so you make it easy to convey your meaning.

When to Post

Most businesses have one of two problems with social media: they can't think of anything to post or they have so much to post that they overwhelm their audience. Neither is a good place to be and can result in a loss of followers, decreased engagement and customers choosing a competitor. You need to establish an appropriate cadence for posting.

What and how often you post is incredibly important. Posting frequency depends on the platforms you're using because each one is a little different. We'll have more on that later, but it's also important to find a sustainable rhythm that works for you. Providing consistency, posting within your niche and finding a frequency that works for your audience are key.

 Rockstar Tips for Planning Social Media

- Draft your content in advance to alleviate the pressure of having to think about what to post every day. This can also help you visualize how frequently you're posting, plan out what types of content to post, gather assets in advance and make sure content is tying into your larger strategic goals. There are a variety of fee-based social media scheduling tools available to draft and automatically post your content like Sprout Social, Hootsuite and Later, but you can also use an Excel spreadsheet as a cost-effective method.

- While social platforms offer free analytics, fee-based tools show additional back-end statistics and analytics to evaluate how your audience is engaging with content. This allows you to see what's working and what's not.

- In times of crisis, you need to be more responsive on social media.

Rockstar Tips for Planning Social Media

- Even when drafting content in advance, don't just set it and forget it. Always review content before posting to ensure it's still relevant and appropriate for that moment in time.

- In addition to spell check and grammar check on your computer, Grammarly is an awesome free tool to help edit social media content along the way.

Unfortunately, there isn't a one-size-fits-all answer to social media frequency, or even what to post. To find the "Goldilocks" answer that's just right, use our recommendations enclosed and your analytics to assess your strategy.

Best Practices Per Channel

 Twitter. Trending as the "information platform," Twitter has been utilized as the tool for real-time information. Use Twitter to update your audience quickly on breaking news, crisis response and more.

- **Frequency.** Twitter moves at lightning speeds and posts get pushed down the feed by other activity in your audience's network quickly, so it's best to post often to keep your brand relevant. Most brands post roughly once per hour.

- **When to Post.** Monday through Friday, 8 a.m. to 4 p.m.
  - The best days are Wednesday and Friday at 9 a.m.
  - The worst day is Saturday.

🐦 Rockstar Tips for Twitter

- Engage more than you broadcast. Ask questions, do polls and be active in public conversations.

- Pay attention to trending topics. This is a simple way to get started. Review the trending topics on Twitter and their hashtags then join the conversation when relevant.

- Use all of your characters. Twitter expanded to 280 characters in 2017, giving you more space to tell your story. We recommend you make every word count with an impactful and relevant message.

- Utilize graphics with text overlays. Set up branded graphic templates to create quote graphics, lists, etc. If you're not a graphic designer, there are tools out there like Canva or Adobe Spark that are easy to use.

- Respond when people "@mention" you. Consumers expect a response from brands and may unfollow you when they don't receive one.

Instagram. Based on sharing photos and videos, Instagram (instagram.com) can be an effective way to show what your company is doing behind the scenes. Engage with your followers by using Instagram Stories to provide quick, in-the-moment updates.

- **Frequency.** Because Instagram relies on images as the main method of communication, it's okay to post more often. Most brands average one to three times per day, but posting once per day is a good place to start.

- **When to Post.** Monday through Friday, 9 a.m. to 4 p.m.
  - The best day is Wednesday at 11 a.m. and Friday from 10 a.m. to 11 a.m.
  - The worst day is Sunday.

Rockstar Tips for Instagram

- Photos first. Instagram is a primarily visual platform, so focus on high-quality, creative photos and graphics to attract the most engagement.

- Captions matter too! Experiment with different caption lengths and see what performs best. Also, consider tying in questions to customers to help spark engagement.

- Don't let your bio go to waste. Your Instagram bio is one of the first things customers see when they visit your page. Make sure it tells your brand story so consumers want to follow you and learn more. Don't forget your website's link too.

⊙ Rockstar Tips for Instagram

- Include location tags, partner mentions and hashtags to increase your discoverability. Hashtags are used to categorize or specify certain topics within the post:
  - When a hashtag is included within a post, if anyone searches that hashtag the photo will appear. This helps expose your brand and posts to new audiences.
  - Incorporate five to 10 hashtags per post.
  - You can also use a branded hashtag to encourage conversation around you and your brand.
- Utilize Instagram Stories to provide real-time updates to your followers. If you need the information to live longer, consider creating a Story Highlight on your profile page.
  - Instagram Stories can also be used to check in with your followers. Use poll and question stickers to learn more about your customers.

Facebook. With more than 1.5 billion active users, it's practically guaranteed your audience, or at least a segment of it, is on Facebook. Trying out different posts is a great way to learn more about your audience, provide customer support and share important information.

- **Frequency.** Most brands post once per day, with a maximum of two posts per day. At a minimum, you should post to Facebook three times per week.
- **When to Post.** Tuesday through Thursday, 8 a.m. to 3 p.m.
  - The best day is Wednesday at 11 a.m. or between 1 p.m. and 2 p.m.
  - The worst day is Sunday.

Rockstar Tips for Facebook

- Create and share creative, high-quality content for the most engagement.

- Try a mix of short and long-form content and see how your audience responds.

- Make sure you have your page set up as a business, not a personal profile.

- Beware of publishing mishaps with page roles. Because your Facebook page is managed through your personal page, make sure you're posting content on behalf of your business, as your business, not as yourself.

- Don't underestimate your profile picture, cover page and account section. These are important components to give new customers a representation of what your page is before they "like" it.

- Don't forget to boost posts, advertise and launch campaigns through Facebook to increase sales and exposure. Facebook has shifted focus to content from friends and family, making it a little harder for businesses, so we highly recommend you put a little money behind your efforts to get yourself noticed.

- Use Insights to determine how your channel is performing and where/when pivots should be made.

- Request reviews by sending new customers an email and asking them to leave you a review on your Facebook page.

- Cross-promote with other businesses you partner with by including a mention in the form of a @company tag or using a hashtag to mention their brand #company.

LinkedIn. LinkedIn is the social media channel of choice for professionals. It's a great place to network with people in your industry. It's also great for marketing your product or service if you're a B2B company.

- **Frequency.** LinkedIn recommends sharing 20 posts per month, which is about one post per business day. Because LinkedIn is a professional networking site, try to stick to posting on traditional business days.
- **When to Post.** Tuesday through Friday, 8 a.m. to 2 p.m.
  - The best days are Wednesday between 8 a.m. and 10 a.m. or noon, Thursday at 9 a.m. or between 1 p.m. and 2 p.m. and Friday at 9 a.m.
  - The worst day is Sunday.

Rockstar Tips for LinkedIn

- Anything you share on LinkedIn should be strictly related to industry news, business announcements and job opportunities.
- LinkedIn makes it easy to write and publish your content, similar to a blog. This is a great way to get yourself noticed as an expert in your field.
- Pay attention to industry trends and provide your thoughts and opinions on the trend.
- Share posts that contain lists, best practices and how-to guides.
- Join in on group discussions, which are like virtual networking events.

NOTE: Recommendations for frequency and when to post are pulled from data gathered by Sprout Social across thousands of social profiles. However, these are general guidelines and can vary based on audience, brand, industry, time of year, etc. The best way to determine what's best for your business is to carefully review analytics and test again and again.

Rockstar Tips for What to Do and Not to Do On Social Media

- **Do...**

  - Be data-driven. Use the insights from your social channels to evaluate engagement from your posts and determine the best time to post, how often to post and which content resonates best with your audience. Make adjustments based on your findings.

  - Keep it short and sweet. Social media isn't meant for writing a novel. People have short attention spans, so keep posts specific and to the point.

  - Tell a visual story. Always include photos, graphics and videos to accompany your posts. A picture is worth a thousand words after all.

  - No designer? No problem! Canva (canva.com) is an excellent source for thousands of professional-looking designs, images and content pieces for both free and premium accounts.

  - Tie in emojis and friendly language to relate to the audience and communicate emotion, if appropriate for your brand.

  - Be consistent. Make a schedule for your content to ensure you're staying active. Posting every once in a blue moon isn't enough.

  - Engage with your audience. Make an effort to check your social feed frequently and respond to questions, comments, testimonials, etc.

  - Cross-promote your channels. If you're on multiple social media platforms, encourage your followers on one platform to check you out on another (just make sure you're providing unique content for them).

  - Add some variety. Different people digest content in different ways. Mix up your content by posting links to articles, images, videos, live feeds, etc.

Rockstar Tips for What to Do and Not to Do On Social Media

- Boost your posts. Social media is no longer "free-to-play." While you don't need a massive budget, a $10 to $20 boost can go a long way to get your content in front of your audience. Don't boost every post, just the ones you really want people to see.

- **Don't...**
  - Skip the plan. It can be easy to get caught up in just posting for the sake of posting but don't forget to stick to your plan and your goals for social media.

  - Be on a platform for the sake of being there. While it can be tempting to join the latest and hottest social media channel, always evaluate if it's worth it for you. Does their audience align with yours? Do you have time to manage another channel? Do you have the right content to post to that channel?

  - Ignore your fans. Remember, social media is meant for building relationships with your followers. Be sure to thank them for their comments, offer them your expertise, etc. You can be a good community or industry partner by engaging with other businesses.

  - Use overly promotional language. Social media is meant to engage and build trust with your followers before you sell to them.

  - Spam your followers with clickbait posts (i.e. "You'll never believe what happened next..."), post the same updates and send private messages when asked to stop.

  - Share too much. There's a fine line between engaging and sharing too much. If you wouldn't share what you're posting with your most important client or customer, don't post it on social media.

  - Be confrontational or vulgar. Social media should be friendly, so don't attack your competitors or yell at your customers. Always stay professional and polite.

Social Media Monitoring and Engaging

Remember when we said before that communication is a two-way street and that social media is all about engagement and relationships? That means posting content to your channels is only part of the equation. You also need to make sure you're monitoring your channels, paying attention to how people are engaging with your content, as well as interacting with your audience and other pages. You should be monitoring and engaging at least once per day, but you might need to do it more frequently depending on the size of your audience, if you're running promotions, and especially during times of crisis when customers may have a lot of questions.

Daily Social Media Checklist

Social media has a lot of moving pieces. Utilize this checklist to make sure you're completing the necessary daily tasks:

☐ Check your notifications for any new comments, mentions and likes.

- Reply to any comments, whether they are positive or negative.
- "Like," "favorite" or "retweet" where appropriate.

☐ Check your inbox for any new direct messages.

- On Instagram, don't forget to check the requests folder too.

☐ Invite people to like your page. You can follow/like new people and pages to grow your audience.

☐ Engage (like, comment, share) with posts from other people and pages to be a good partner in the social community.

☐ Double-check your most recent posts.
  • Check for relevance (situations can change overnight).
  • Check all links to make sure they work.
  • Check for typos.

☐ Double-check your upcoming posts, especially if you're scheduling content in advance, to ensure they're still relevant and proofed.

☐ Check your paid promotions if you're running them.
  • How are they performing?
  • Is your audience engaging?
  • Are you still within your budget?

Analytics

The world of social media is constantly changing and evolving. Science and technology; global and local economies; audience preferences; and crises all shape the landscape of social media. Keep track of customer engagement with analytics and trends in usage and adapt your marketing plan to be a step ahead. Most social channels have analytics built right into the tool, commonly called Insights, making it easy to see how your content is performing on each channel. If you want a one-stop-shop, there are also fee-based programs that will bring the data from all your social channels together into one spot. Sprout Social, Hootsuite and Later are all popular options, but there are others as well. Below are some analytics to track to make the best data-driven decisions for your marketing:

Impressions. Total number of times any content from your page was seen in a news feed or by visits to your page.

Reach. Total number of unique people who saw your content.

Post Engagements. Total number of comments, shares or reactions to your post.

 Engagement Rate. The rate of engagements per impression or reach.

 Link Clicks. Total number of clicks on links with your content. Excludes other clicks such as photos, videos or post-expansion clicks.

 Organic Likes. Total number of users who liked your page by organic (unpaid) reach.

 Net Likes. Total number of paid or organic likes minus the number of unlikes.

 Total Fans. Total number of users who liked your page from the last day of the reporting period.

Rockstar Tip for Analytics

As you can see, there are a lot of analytics you can track and measure but focus on the ones that matter to you and your goals. If you're focused on traffic or conversions, you might want to pay more attention to link clicks versus page likes. Or, if you're focused on building a strong community, you might want to pay closer attention to your engagement rate instead of impressions.

Here are some examples of how to showcase your great work and ensure you are reaching your goals:

Tracking Value

Channel	Campaign	Return on Impressions (ROI)
Online Advertising	Campaign name	Impressions, clicks, click-through rate
Sponsorships & Events	Event name	Number of attendees, new clients, eNewsletter sign-ups, follow ups
eNewsletters	Dates sent	Number of recipients, open rate, click-through rates, # of calls or responses
Public Relations	Press release/ pitch	Number of outlets targeted, media pick-up, circulation, online monthly visitors
Website Traffic	Promotion name	Number of online visitors, click-throughs to your website, eNewsletter sign-ups, form completion
Social Media	Campaign name	Likes, comments, engagements, impressions, shares, retweets, click-throughs to your website

Rockstar Tip for Tracking Value

Use tracking codes on links (embedded) to track referrals. You can track these through Google Analytics (where you can see how many views/clicks links get). Or, create a Bit.ly link and enter the full URL in the box, click "Shorten" and you'll be taken to a page with your new shorter URL. Then copy and paste it into your social media posts, blog copy and more to track!

The importance of continuous testing cannot be overstated. Our Rockstars encourage you to consistently track results and leverage measurement tools to make stronger data-driven decisions.

CRISIS COMMUNICATIONS
cri·sis com·mun·i·ca·tions | noun

The plan you'll be glad you put together if $#!+ hits the fan.

We've saved the best, or worst, for last. No one goes looking for a crisis, but sometimes it finds you. When it does, it pays to be prepared.

Crisis communications is an important subset of public relations. It is a process designed to lessen the damage an unplanned difficulty can inflict on a business and its stakeholders. A crisis communications plan ensures that all personnel can promptly and effectively communicate during an event; share information that will allow the organization to quickly rectify the situation; protect employees and assets; and secure business continuity.

A crisis can take many forms, such as an employee issue or injury, compromised information or a damaging online review. Those who remain calm, cool and collected when a crisis hits will have the best chance to maintain their message, brand and image. A crisis can be an opportunity for you to establish your credibility and show your audience your true colors.

If you don't already have a crisis management program, here are a few tips to help get you started:

Rockstar Tips for Crisis Management

Why should you care?

Crisis always hits when you least expect it.

Crisis can quickly damage the brand you've worked so hard to build.

Crisis news travels fast, especially with social media, so it's important to be as proactive as possible.

Best practices

Tell the truth.

Take accountability.

Address the situation quickly.

Tell your audience what you're doing about it.

Silence is not golden, avoid "no comment."

Consult your legal team or lawyer.

Questions to ask

What are the big risks for my business? How will I combat them?

If these things happen do they require internal and/or external communication?

Who is the crisis communication team? What are their roles?

How do I mitigate future crisis?

The most important thing that any business can do in a crisis is to stay in touch with customers or, in the case of an employee issue, your team. It's important to keep the lines of communication open and to keep your communications up to date.

During a crisis, or before one ever strikes, we recommend reviewing and documenting the following five steps.

STEP 1:

Establish a crisis communication team

The only way to stay organized under pressure is by planning ahead and knowing in advance who will take the lead in a crisis, who is the backup if that person is out of reach and who will be a spokesperson should your company need to comment to the press. This should be documented and distributed throughout your organization. Depending on your organization's product or service, you may also need to pull in other key personnel to the team, such as facilities, security, IT, financial, etc. Make sure all key contacts are saved in your cell phone and you have after-hours information, because, unfortunately, that's when crises often happen.

STEP 2:

Map out holding statements so you can quickly communicate

Customers need to know how they can get in touch with you, and there's nothing more frustrating than not being able to find that information. You'll want to be sure to communicate information such as whether or not you're still open, if you've changed how you're conducting business, what has changed for your business and customers (i.e. hours of operation) and how you're addressing the crisis. In the case of an employee issue, be ready to provide a high-level update to other employees as soon as it's appropriate.

To be prepared, map out the most common incidents that may occur and write a corresponding holding statement, which is a prepared statement with information about what you know and how you will respond during a crisis (see example later in this chapter). Consider creating up to three different versions with blanks for the details. You will need to customize the statement before actually publishing it, but having something drafted in advance will give you a solid starting point should a crisis occur.

STEP 3:

Distribute the information

You'll also want to determine in advance the best communication channels for distributing the holding statement, including internal communication, as well as a point person who is responsible for the information being posted in the right places.

Your team should know first. The last thing you want is for an employee to find out about your company crisis in the news as they are sipping their morning coffee. This leads to a lack of trust and more internal issues than you can imagine. Make sure to let employees know what happened; what is being distributed to the public and when; as well as who they should direct questions to as they arise. Having a good internal alert system in place will ensure that your message is accurate and your reputation stays intact.

Consider setting a threshold for what constitutes sending out a message to your customers. Make sure that the message impacts them and matters. Sending unnecessary communications can irritate people and you may risk damaging your reputation.

For distribution, we recommend using as many channels as possible to ensure you're reaching your customers in a variety of ways. For example, add a notice to your website, pin a post to the top of your Facebook page, update your Google My Business page and send out an email to your customers. Make sure your messaging is consistent across all the platforms and that you are quick to respond to any questions. Remember, social media moves quickly.

STEP 4:

Keep communication going

Communication is not a one-and-done process. It's important to keep the communication going as often as you can, without over-communicating to the point of fatigue, to maintain a connection with your customers and keep them up to date on what's happening. With an employee issue, it may be helpful to send out a longer follow up after the dust has settled to outline next steps. Stay in control of the message as much as possible. Keeping these efforts going pays off in the long run and sets you up for a successful post-crisis recovery. People remember the businesses that were present, even during a pandemic, recession or unforeseen event.

We recommend starting with the communication channels you already have set up and then consider adding new tools to your toolkit over time that can help you communicate even better to customers. Think about utilizing social media, messaging apps, emails, blogs, PR, your website, etc. Strong customer relationships driven by thoughtful and relevant messaging will win in the end.

Don't forget to engage with your customers. If people are posting about your business, be as responsive as you can by answering questions, thanking them for their support, responding to comments with updates and getting information to them quickly.

STEP 5:

Maintain your marketing efforts

A lot of businesses make the mistake of pulling back and slashing PR and marketing during tough times. They assume their customers will still be there when they return, but that often isn't the case. If you're not doing it, your competitors will.

By making strategic decisions and maintaining communication even during a crisis, you can emerge stronger. Remember to remain flexible in your PR and marketing efforts. You may need to shift your messaging, channels and even objectives but maintaining your communication will keep you in front of your customers.

Crisis Communication Plan

Crisis Communication Team & Roles

(1) Crisis communication lead notifies the crisis communication team.

- Crisis communication lead should get the facts, judge the validity based on the source of information and attempt to discern the magnitude of the event.

- If needed, the team will convene or hold a conference call to assess impact, determine next steps, messaging and assign/clarify roles.

- If this is an employee issue, consult with an HR professional as additional steps may need to be taken.

(2) Crisis communication lead issues a holding statement to employees and, depending on the level of the crisis and who is affected, business partners, local officials and the media. See the definitions section for more about holding statements.

- The designated spokesperson for the crisis should handle all questions from employees, the public or media.

(3) Crisis communication lead, or another member of the team, will continue to provide updates as needed to affected groups.

(4) Social media lead will distribute messaging on social media platforms.

(5) Once the crisis is over, the recovery plan goes into effect.

As you are filling out your crisis team, consider other business partners (lawyer, IT consultant, bookkeeper, CPA, business coach, HR, etc.) who would need to be involved in the situation. Collect all the information in one spot.

Role	Name (first/last)	Company	Title	Cell	Office	Email
Crisis communication lead						
Crisis communication backup						
Company spokesperson						
(Add more if needed)						

Visit www.wildrockpr.com/ready-to-rock or contact us at readytorock@wildrockpr.com for your FREE printable templates, checklists and forms to take notes as you read.

Change. Adapt. Rock.
WildRock Public Relations & Marketing®

Holding Statements

- What do employees, media or customers want to know?

  - What happened? _____
    _____

  - Who is in charge? _____
    _____

  - Who was hurt? _____
    _____

  - What happens next? _____
    _____

  - What are you doing about it? _____
    _____

  - Why did this happen? _____
    _____

  - Did you have forewarning? _____
    _____

Example: A [what happened] at [location] involving [who] occurred [when] at [time]. The incident is under investigation and more information is forthcoming.

Change. Adapt. Rock.
WildRock Public Relations & Marketing®

Visit www.wildrockpr.com/ready-to-rock or contact us at readytorock@wildrockpr.com for your FREE printable templates, checklists and forms to take notes as you read.

Distribution Checklist

- [ ] Internal protocol, such as an email or company meeting.
- [ ] Business partner or key stakeholders, likely personal phone calls or an email.
- [ ] Media, likely emails with a press announcement or holding statement.
- [ ] Website, add an update or press announcement to the homepage.
- [ ] Social media, create a post to share the holding statement.
- [ ] Email, if you have an email program already, you can use this to update customers on the situation.
- [ ] Online listings, similar to social media, are places such as Google, Yahoo or Yelp where you can create a post to promote your businesses' holding statement.

Ongoing Updates

Use the checklist below to keep the information updated as the incident either progresses or resolves itself.

- [ ] Update employees and stakeholders daily.
- [ ] Update the website weekly.
- [ ] Post daily/weekly on social media (depending on the severity of the situation).
- [ ] Respond promptly to questions.
- [ ] Send customer emails with new information every one to two weeks (depending on the severity of the situation).
- [ ] Issue a statement to the media once the issue is resolved. Consider personal follow ups to media who ran stories to let them know it's been resolved.

Recovery Plan

We recommend developing a recovery plan to ensure the business can resume operations soon after the crisis occurs.

Recovery Plan Checklist:

☐ Obtain feedback and conduct crisis evaluation.

- Analyze feedback from employees, customers and media coverage. You could do this through a survey and by analyzing media coverage, both in terms of quantity and sentiment.
- Run through the ROCKS exercise (included in the marketing strategy chapter).
- Solicit feedback from your team and employees.
- Keep your crisis communication plan updated. Add relevant information to your crisis communications when appropriate.

☐ Rebuild your brand by providing value-added content or educating the public on what you learned from your crisis.

☐ Promote the company's capabilities and value by staying active on your marketing channels and focusing on what your company does best.

☐ Continue to monitor public opinion, media and business partners so you can quickly correct any misinformation that may still be circulating.

NEED CRISIS COMMUNICATION EXPERTS?

WildRock's Rockstars are here to help solve your biggest crisis communication challenges. Learn more at www.wildrockpr.com.

CONCLUSION
con·clu·si·on | noun

Where the rubber meets the road and the real work begins.

While we could dedicate hundreds more pages to this book, this should give you enough information and direction to get started with effective and successful marketing. Wading into the waters of PR and marketing can be murky and downright difficult at times, but with this guide as your lifeboat, you can navigate the twists and turns that come with communications. Just keep in mind, these tools and tactics can be more of an art form than an equation and may require tweaks and changes along the way.

You are now ready to:

 Rock your public relations
Build and maintain relationships with other organizations, the media and the public to better communicate your story.

 Dive into digital marketing
Connect with and learn about your customers, promote your brand and grow your business.

 Create rockstar content
Make your message stand out by providing information, adding value and letting your customers know that you understand their needs.

Navigate social media
Analyze a platform's performance and use analytics to optimize your content.

 Build a solid strategy
Streamline your goals, improve efficiency, provide a measurement for success and move your business forward.

These core aspects of marketing can help your business in challenging times and beyond. Adaptability in business is crucial for moving forward and being one step ahead. We recommend reviewing these tools regularly and keeping your plan updated. Being proactive will pay dividends in the long run, enabling you to pivot on short notice.

Remember, what works today may not work tomorrow, so always keep an eye on the horizon. If we can support you along the way, we are here for you and ready to rock!

Stay connected with us for more insights on our blog and social media channels.

 facebook.com/WildRockPublicRelations

 twitter.com/wildrockpr

 instagram.com/wildrockprandmarketing

 linkedin.com/company/wildrock-public-relations-and-marketing

 wildrockpr.com

NOTES

What were my biggest "ah-has?"

_____

_____

_____

_____

_____

How will I stay up to speed with marketing?

_____

_____

_____

_____

_____

What areas am I comfortable in taking on myself, delegating or what should I consider outsourcing?

_____

_____

_____

_____

_____

What areas of this book do I need to re-read?

_____

_____

_____

_____

_____

What are 3 actions I can take right now?

_____

_____

_____

_____

_____

Other thoughts:

_____

_____

_____

_____

_____

_____

_____

_____

_____

_____

_____

_____

_____

THANKS FOR READING!

If you enjoyed Change. Adapt. Rock. please consider leaving an honest review on your favorite store.

Change. Adapt. Rock.
WildRock Public Relations & Marketing®

MARKETING DEFINED

- **A/B testing** – Also known as split testing or bucket testing, A/B testing is a method of using two versions of a web page, email or another marketing asset to analyze the difference in performance.

- **Ad creative** - A format that provides an outline of information and contains all of the visual content for creating an ad.

- **Advertising** - Paid techniques used to draw attention to your awesome products, services, opinions or causes to encourage a response.

- **Advertorial** - Using an editorial or journalistic style ad to share information about a product.

- **Alt tag** – HTML attribute or description applied to image tags that talks directly to search engines.

- **Analyst** - A person who studies numbers from data and discerns what they mean.

- **AP Style** - The Associated Press agency's fancy grammar, capitalization and punctuation recommendations used by news and media channels.

- **AP Stylebook** - A compilation of design and procedure guidelines developed for news writing.

- **Augmented Reality (AR)** - Technology that creates virtual emersion in a computer-generated environment.

- **Backlinks** - When one website links to another.

- **Blog** - A collection of articles, as part of a website, that generally relates to a specific topic to provide information, personal experience or opinion.

- **Blogger** - A writer who provides material for blog posts.
- **Boilerplate** - Standardized wording at the end of a press release that describes who you are at a high level. It should include the most important facts about your brand including where you are located, when you started, what you do, what makes you different and a link to your website.
- **Brand asset** - Key indicators that identify your brand and its values and make it easily recognizable to consumers. Includes logo, image, video and more.
- **Brand awareness** - How much consumers know about your company's character and unique qualities.
- **Brand exposure** – Any opportunity to promote your business and reach new audiences.
- **Budget** – Defined estimate of projected costs you want to invest.
- **Call to action** - Text designed to prompt readers for a quick response. Actions could include visit website, call, book, etc.
- **Campaign** - A creative and structured plan of marketing activities developed to accomplish set goals.
- **CAN-SPAM laws** - An outline of regulations for commercial e-mail. These laws detail stipulations for messages, provide recipients the choice to opt-out and specify consequences for those who can't stop sending junk mail.
- **Canva** - Canva is a graphic design platform that allows users to create social media graphics, presentations, posters and other visual content.
- **Case study** - An analysis of a specific scenario to provide information and insight for the future.
- **Channels** - An information or communication network such as Facebook, Instagram, email, website, etc.
- **Chatbots and messenger** - Applications, generally programmed to use artificial intelligence, that encourages individual communication with customers.

- **Chatfuel** - Free/paid program for chatbot setups.
- **Circulation** – The count of how many copies of a particular publication are distributed.
- **Click-through rate** - The ratio of users who click on a specific link from an email, web page, advertisement, etc. Commonly used to measure the success of online advertising and the effectiveness of email campaigns.
- **Co-marketing** - Brands with similar goals who join forces to promote a shared effort.
- **Competitive analysis** – Identifying major competitors and researching their products, sales, marketing and more to understand and keep an eye on what they are doing.
- **Content marketing** – Creating and sharing consumable material such as videos, blogs, social media and more to stimulate interest and stay in front of your target audience.
- **Conversion rate** - The percentage of people who complete the desired goal after seeing an advertisement.
- **Coverage type** – The form of earned media received from PR efforts including feature, mention, roundup, video or press release.
- **Coverage views** - The number of people who have seen or read your earned media coverage.
- **Crisis communications** - A preparedness plan for businesses in the event of an unexpected or unfavorable scenario.
- **CRM/PRM** – Like a traditional customer relationship management tool that organizes customer interactions and activities, a public relations management tool unites the PR workflow in one system to track media outreach and communication efforts.
- **Cross-promotion** - A technique to partner with another company to promote each other's products or services to a new audience.
- **Customer persona** - A model with your target audience's key traits that helps marketers connect customer expectations with the product or service provider's assumptions.

- **Dateline** – Denotes the time and place a press release is created and distributed. Typically included in the first line before the first sentence.

- **Differentiators** - Something that provides a notable distinction.

- **Digital marketing** - Using online interactive programs to electronically engage with consumers.

- **Directory listing** – Online business listing that provides pertinent information in a profile such as description, hours of operation, location, directions and website.

- **Domain authority** - A website's classification for a subject matter or industry that affects search rankings through automated algorithms.

- **Earned media coverage** - Content that is authored and shared by a traditional news source that resulted from PR outreach and is not paid.

- **Email marketing** - Utilizing electronic mail to provide information about your company, product or service to customers to promote loyalty, confidence and brand awareness.

- **Email newsletter** - Content intended to keep customers updated on business happenings consistently. Email newsletters are less promotional and more educational. The aim is to make your brand more recognizable and cohesive.

- **Embargo** – A request or requirement that news is held and not published until a specific day and time.

- **Embedded links** - A hyperlink on text or photo that takes you to a website.

- **Engagement rate** - The rate of engagements per impression or reach.

- **Executive summary** - A synopsis to provide key information in a high-level overview.

- **Facebook** - A social media platform allowing users to create profiles, connect with others, share information and photos.

- **Facebook Creator Studio** - Creator Studio brings together all the tools you need to effectively post, manage, monetize and measure content across all your Facebook pages and Instagram accounts.

- **Grammarly** - A computer program that utilizes artificial intelligence and language processing to correct grammar and spelling. It can provide advanced writing assistance such as clarity, style and tone.

- **H1** – Main and first header tag on a web page, also the most important header when it comes to SEO. H1 tags should contain the page's keyword or keyword phrase.

- **Headline** - Text at the top of a document generally concise and applicable to the content.

- **Hi-res images** - Detailed and clear photographs, art or other types of digital images.

- **Holding statement** - A short statement submitted to the media as soon as a crisis has occurred that includes what happened and what you're doing about it.

- **Hootsuite** - A program designed to manage social media interactions across different channels using one interface.

- **Impressions** - Total number of times any content from your page was seen in a news feed or by visits to your page

- **In-kind donation** - Transfer of a non-cash asset to a 5019(c)(3) charity.

- **Industry thought leader** - A person who shares expertise and unique perspective on an industry with others.

- **Influencer** - A person or organization that has maintained an expert level of knowledge or social impact to affect their audience's decisions.

- **Instagram** - A social media channel connecting users through shared images and videos.

- **Internal communications** - Dialogue and information transfer within a business.

- **Inverted pyramid** - A model used to depict how to prioritize information with the most important items at the beginning followed by supporting details.

- **Key messages** - Specific phrases you want your audience to remember from your content.

- **Key performance indicators** - A value used to measure the success of a business by achieving quantifiable performance goals.

- **Lifecycle stage** - Offering your audience the experiences they need, want or like as they progress from prospects to customers to advocates.

- **Link clicks** - Total number of clicks on links within your content.

- **LinkedIn** - A social network centered around business and employment where users can network, search for jobs and share information.

- **Listicle** - Content partially or entirely in list form.

- **Lookalike audience** - Method of engaging bigger audiences from smaller target characteristics to increase reach for marketers.

- **MailChimp** - Platform used to help businesses automate and manage e-mail marketing.

- **ManyChat** - Free/paid program for chatbot setups.

- **Media** – Mass media institutions such as newspapers, magazines, radio, TV broadcast, podcasts, blogs and websites.

- **Media database** – A directory of journalists, reporters, editors and other media contacts that includes profile information such as publication they write for, beat/interest area, contact information and more.

- **Media mention** – When your brand is referenced briefly in the media.

- **Media outlets** - Distribution channels that provide publications or news to the public.

- **Messenger** - A program used to communicate on an individual basis with customers.
- **Metrics** - A specification of measurement.
- **Net likes** - Total number of paid or organic likes minus the number of un-likes.
- **Networking events** - Opportunity to connect with other individuals and companies to build better business relationships.
- **News coverage** – Representation of your brand by a traditional news outlet such as a magazine, newspaper or blog.
- **News distribution** - Spreading event coverage to the public through different media outlets.
- **News hook** – The angle for your press release or pitch that will intrigue and captivate readers and the media.
- **Newsroom** - Location of writing and editing for news or broadcasting.
- **Newswire** – A service used to distribute press releases quickly to a large audience of media.
- **Newsworthiness** - Stories or events that are notable for distribution to the media.
- **Objectives** - Goals you aim to achieve.
- **Online readership** - Number of people who read content on the web.
- **Open rate** - The percentage of people who "view" your e-mail.
- **Organic likes** - Total number of users who like your page by unpaid reach.
- **Paid advertising** - Purchasing online ad space to advertise your product or service.
- **Pay-per-click advertising (PPC)** - Online ad space purchased only when the ad is clicked by an internet user.
- **Pinterest** - Photo/video-sharing social media platform for viewing and saving information about certain areas of interest.

- **Pitching** – The act of sharing concise and compelling information with the media to get them interested in a topic or story. Typically sent via email, but it can be done in person or over the phone.

- **Pixel** – A basic unit of color used in design programs like Adobe Photoshop as well as computer monitors, oftentimes used to describe the size of online banners and ad creative.

- **Placements** – Another way to describe news coverage (see news coverage above).

- **Platforms** - Technology that allows for the creation, launch and management of social media applications.

- **Post engagements** - Total number of comments, shares or reactions to your post.

- **Press release** - A statement released to the media providing information about a specific topic.

- **Public relations** – A strategic communication process that builds mutually beneficial relationships between organizations and their publics.

- **Reach** - Total number of unique people who saw your content.

- **Referral traffic** - Online users who accessed your website, without using a search engine, through a different website.

- **Reporting** – Measuring progress to showcase value, success and identify steps to pivot or improve marketing performance to meet goals.

- **Retargeting** - A method of reminding customers about your products and services after they leave your site without making a purchase.

- **Return on investment (ROI)** - The proportion of net profit over time and investment cost used to evaluate the effectiveness of an investment.

- **Retweet** - On Twitter, a retweet is reposting another user's tweet on your profile to share with your followers.

- **ROCKS exercise** – A practice to help determine the crucial path forward for marketing your business by analyzing patterns and similarities.

- **Search engine marketing (SEM)** - Increasing brand awareness by promoting your website through search engine results.

- **Search engine optimization (SEO)** - Website content and structure built to achieve a better ranking in search engine results.

- **SEC requirements** - A law requiring business investors to be updated on financial and other important information regarding securities presented for public purchase and forbidding deception, falsification, and other fraud in the transaction of securities.

- **Sentiment** - Overall attitude or thought in response to a situation. The sentiment can be positive, neutral or negative.

- **Share of voice** - The percentage of interaction your business has with customers versus the competition for the same target audience.

- **Shoppable post** – An interactive way to tag products in a social media post to encourage shopping directly from the platform.

- **Smart bidding** - Automated bid management software to assist businesses in finding the best online ad space for optimal conversions for the lowest price.

- **SMART goals** - Specific, measurable, attainable, realistic and time-based objectives.

- **Social media** - Online programs designed for information sharing and to encourage interaction between users.

- **Social media followers** – The number of individuals who subscribe to your social media channels.

- **Social media marketing** - Using social media applications to connect with your target audience and build brand awareness.

- **Social shares** - Users who repost your content to their profile and distribute your information to their followers.

- **Sponsored content** - A paid form of marketing where material, provided by an advertiser, is posted on separate publications with a similar style to coincide with the company's editorial content.

- **Sponsorships** - A public relations tactic that provides exposure to target audiences.
- **Sprout** - An all-inclusive social media management program with one user interface for posting, correspondence and analytics across various channels.
- **Stakeholders** - People most affected by the state of the business.
- **Strategy** - A well-planned and a goal-oriented path forward.
- **Subhead** - The supporting title text below the headline.
- **SWOT** - The study of a company's development to determine its strengths, weaknesses, opportunities, and threats.
- **Tactics** - Methods used to accomplish your goals.
- **Target audience** - A group of people identified to be most interested in your service or product.
- **Target markets** - Ideal groups of customers for the business or organization to focus marketing efforts on.
- **Third-party validation** - Utilizing an unaffiliated expert to validate information about another business.
- **Total fans** - The combined number of users who like and follow your social media channels.
- **Trade publications** - A collection of content featuring information about a specific area or industry.
- **Tradeshows** - An event featuring a variety of organizations, within an industry, to exhibit their products and services with others for educational purposes, networking and sales.
- **Traditional media outlets** - Types of mass media, such as magazines, newspapers, radio, TV and websites that provide news to the public.
- **Twitter** - A social network channel that encourages user interaction through posting and "retweeting" information in short-form posts.
- **Unique monthly views** - The number of people, only counted once, who have visited your website per month.

- **URL** - An address for a specific web location.

- **User Generated Content (UGC)** - Generally unpaid text, images, video or audio created and published by a consumer to promote a service, product or associated business.

- **Value proposition** - Unique brand identifier that provides a clear and concise statement to consumers about what they can expect from the company.

- **Wish list outlet** - A key media outlet where you would like to see placement.

- **Word-of-mouth marketing** - A free type of advertising from customers sharing their positive experiences with your product or service by encouragement from your business or organically.

Made in the USA
Middletown, DE
04 September 2020